Praise
Heartfelt L

00700618

"What parent hasn't wrestled with the discipline dilemma? Clay Clarkson offers us a biblical model of discipline that shapes a child's character without destroying the child's spirit. Does he make house calls?"

—CHUCK BORSELLINO, PH.D., PSY.D., author
of *How to Raise Totally Awesome Kids* and host
of *At Home Live with Chuck & Jenni*

"*Heartfelt Discipline* is not so much a roadmap as it is a compass for navigating the path of Christian parenthood. Clay Clarkson shows you how to get off the crowded freeway of rat-race parenting and explore the scenic highways of family life. He helps you avoid the hazards and enjoy the highlights along the way."

—BUDDY OWENS, author of *The Way of a Worshiper*
and general editor of *The NIV Worship Bible*

"This is the best biblical foundation for child discipline that I have seen. Clay uses Scripture to define Christian parenting, clarifying common misconceptions and teaching parents how to touch a child's heart instead of relying on typical parenting formulas. Every parent should use this book as a theological basis for raising children."

—DR. SCOTT TURANSKY, president of the National Center
for Biblical Parenting and author of *Say Goodbye
to Whining, Complaining, and Bad Attitudes...in You
and Your Kids*

Heart*felt*
DISCIPLINE

Heart*felt*

THE GENTLE ART *of* TRAINING *and* GUIDING YOUR CHILD

DISCIPLINE

CLAY CLARKSON

WATERBROOK
PRESS

HEARTFELT DISCIPLINE
PUBLISHED BY WATERBROOK PRESS
2375 Telstar Drive, Suite 160
Colorado Springs, Colorado 80920
A division of Random House, Inc.

ISBN 1-57856-583-9

Printed in the United States of America
2003—First Edition

10 9 8 7 6 5 4 3 2 1

This book is dedicated to my children:
Sarah, Joel, Nathan, and Joy

Thank you all for being the laboratory for heartfelt discipline —
and especially for enduring the times when it was more felt than heart.
I love you and enjoy every step that we walk together along God's path of life.
—Dad

CONTENTS

DISCIPLINE THAT TOUCHES THE HEART

Solving the Discipline Puzzle

As Christian parents, we are sure of one thing: If we are to honor God's design for the family, we have no choice but to discipline our children. But ask Christian parents to define *discipline,* and you'll quickly find there is little agreement on what it means, how it should be done, at what age, or to what ends. Probe a little deeper, and you'll uncover real puzzlement over the dreaded *D* word of parenting.

More often than not, the responsibility to discipline our children causes us frustration, worry, guilt, and even heartache. We want our children to develop godly character and bedrock faith. But when it comes to discipline, we're looking at a puzzle that becomes harder to solve with each stage of our children's development. The pieces just don't seem to fit together no matter how hard we try, and the picture remains unclear.

One reason for the uncertainty is that we tend to confuse discipline with punishment. The notion that every sinful and childish infraction must meet with strict punishment to prevent a child from becoming a little rebel is a heavy burden for parents to carry. And, even more, it's a heavy burden for our children to endure. Though *loving punishment* is clearly a biblical teaching, it seems more like an emotional oxymoron when it comes to children. Feeling an urgency to punish casts a gray cloud over our

2 + DISCIPLINE THAT TOUCHES THE HEART

parenting, making discipline an onerous duty rather than a challenging journey for us to take with our children. While punishment is one component of the Bible's view of childhood discipline, it is only *one* aspect of a much bigger picture.

Contrary to popular thinking, the biblical picture of discipline for young children is not found in the polarized positions of either "hands-off" permissiveness or "hands-on" authoritarianism. Instead, it is found in the relational, "hands-around" perspective that comes through clearly in Scripture. The hands-around approach puts parents in the role of loving and godly guides who direct, correct, and protect their children as they walk together on the path of life. This portrait comes through most clearly in the book of Proverbs, but it is underscored throughout Scripture.

In this book, I call this biblical perspective *heartfelt discipline.* This bigger-picture, biblical view of discipline is not found in God's isolated acts of correction or admonishing His people. Instead, it comes into view when we step back to see the special love relationship between parent and child that God intends. This picture of discipline is truly heart-to-heart. The chapters that follow will prepare you to implement this approach, first by taking a fresh look at what the Bible teaches about childhood and discipline, and then by offering practical suggestions in three crucial areas: directing, correcting, and protecting your children. You will realize that God has not provided a step-by-step process for discipline. Instead, discipline is something parents do at all times and in every place (see Deuteronomy 6:4-9). And as we direct, correct, and protect our children, we are training and instructing our children in the way of righteousness, what Solomon called the path of life (see Proverbs 4:18; 15:24).

This book, therefore, does not outline a foolproof, how-to formula that promises to make your life easier. But it does offer a more satisfying and biblically consistent picture of how God wants you to guide your young children through childhood and into maturity. With our problem-solving mind-set, we often are tempted to rely more on experts or even our own ingenuity than on God and His Word when disciplining our children. Rather than providing neatly wrapped packages of biblical instructions, though, the Scriptures seek to teach us wisdom so we can lead our children on the path of life.[1] God wants us to be effective parents, but even more He wants us to be wise parents.

In the pages of this book, I hope to open your eyes to the heart of God, to the hearts of your children, and to your own heart. There is great freedom and confidence in Spirit-led, faith-based discipline, but it's a direction you and I must choose. As we apply the wisdom of Scripture, the pieces of the discipline puzzle begin to fall into place, and the picture becomes complete.

Heartfelt Discipline offers a way of thinking about children and about childhood discipline that will change their hearts, but even more it will change ours. As we explore what the Bible teaches about children, parents, and discipline, I invite you to begin a new journey—walking together with your children on God's path of life. So I encourage you to turn the page and begin the adventure of applying God's heart-changing wisdom to the way you guide, instruct, and discipline your children.

PART I

HEARTFELT

DISCIPLINE

CHAPTER 1

THE HEART
OF PARENTHOOD

The Bible's Liberating Truth About Discipline

Watch over your heart with all diligence,

For from it flow the springs of life.

PROVERBS 4:23

Christian parenting is a journey. The destination is clear—raising godly children—but the roads to get there are not always clearly marked. We have God's perfect road map, the Bible, but He has not taken a divine highlighter pen and marked the single route that leads to where we want to go. He expects us to study the map and chart a wise course to the desired destination.

In my own experience as a parent, I quickly learned that the road I select for childhood discipline determines what the journey will be like. Fortunately, God gives us the freedom to change our itinerary along the way. In fact, my journey has included a couple of major directional changes in order to get my family on the road we now travel. In these first few chapters, we will look at those directional changes and then identify the roads that make the journey of parenting rewarding and even enjoyable.

As our first child, Sarah, moved into toddlerhood and beyond, I pictured my responsibility as a Christian parent as being a kind of gardener for God. Whenever I helped Sarah learn to pick up her toys, I saw myself planting a seed of orderliness and responsibility in her heart. When I corrected her for not obeying quickly when I asked her to come to me, I was planting a seed of respect for authority. When I helped train her to do her work carefully and thoroughly, I was planting a seed of self-control. When I talked to her about a scripture and prayed with her, I was planting seeds of devotion. All of these seeds, I thought, would take root and one day blossom into godly character. I felt it was my responsibility to plant the seeds and water them, and God would make them grow. As Sarah grew up, her life would be a garden producing fruitful plants and beautiful flowers, all emerging from the seeds I had helped plant in her heart.

But over time it became clear that there was much more going in than these good seeds. Like weeds that corrupt a beautiful garden, sin grew in Sarah's heart, just as it does in every person. It took a lot of extra work to keep the weedy sin from choking out the good seeds. No matter how hard my wife, Sally, and I tried to guard Sarah against negative influences, the not-so-good seeds found their way into our daughter's heart. And, much to my dismay, I could see some of my own areas of sinfulness mirrored in the life of my child.

I realized that if Sarah's godly character depended on my planting enough good seeds in her heart, all would be lost. It's no secret around our house that I'm not a good gardener in real life—I'm allergic to yard work. Likewise, I didn't feel like a very good heart gardener either. I didn't want to settle for growing a pretty good garden in my daughter's heart, but bountiful and fruitful seemed beyond my capabilities. And with all the negative influences in the world, how could I ever hope to plant enough good seeds to choke out the negative? If the quality of my parenting were ultimately to be judged by whether I won the battle between good and bad influences, then I was defeated before I even began.

My perspective changed, though, when I read again what Jesus had to say about seed sowing. Something stood out that I hadn't seen before, and it helped me make sense of the early years of my children's lives. In fact, it completely changed the way I perceived my role as a parent and helped arrange the pieces of the parenting puzzle in a way that made sense. His words brought together God's requirements for parents not only in the area of discipline, but also in the way we look at and relate to our children.

SEEDS AND SOILS

It's easy to read the parable of the sower with a kind of lazy familiarity. Yet any parable that is recorded in such detail in all three synoptic gospels (Matthew, Mark, and Luke) demands closer attention. I've always preferred Luke's version because it is so succinct and clear, especially his record of Jesus' explanation of what the parable means. To quickly recount, Jesus described a sower going out to sow his seed, the different kinds of ground the seed falls upon, and what happens to the seed in each instance. In each of the three accounts, Jesus stopped after telling the parable to the gathered crowds and turned to respond to His disciples' questions. He explained what each part of His parable means.

Here's the digest version from Luke 8. The seed is the Word of God. It's the message of the kingdom and the gospel of salvation. Seed that falls along the roadside and is trampled and eaten by birds represents those people who hear God's Word, but the devil "takes away the word from their heart, so that they will not believe and be saved" (verse 12). Seed that falls on rocky soil and quickly grows but then withers for lack of water represents those people who "receive the word with joy" and believe for a while, but who fall away in a time of temptation for lack of root (verse 13). Seed that falls among the thicket of choking thorns represents those people who hear God's Word, but as they continue on the road of life, the "worries and riches and pleasures of this life" overcome the Word, and they never grow to fruitful maturity (verse 14).

It's the final seed story that catches my attention, though—the seed that fell into good soil, which "grew up, and produced a crop a hundred times as great" (verse 8). Jesus said that this seed represents those people who "have heard the word in an honest and good heart, and hold it fast, and bear fruit with perseverance" (verse 15). I can't read that passage without thinking, *This is what I want for my children—that they would hear the truth of God, hold it fast, be spiritually fruitful, and persevere in their faith.* I want my children to be bountiful and fruitful for God! My response, then, must be to sow as much of the seed of God's Word in my children's hearts as I can. It's all about sowing seeds…isn't it?

Maybe not. Four words in verse 15 changed my way of thinking both about seed sowing and about my children. Look at the words Jesus used to describe the good soil. The seed of God's Word fell on soil described as an "honest and good heart." This soil was receptive to God's Word *before* the life-changing seed of the gospel found root there. Jesus seemed to be saying that a heart, prior to being "saved" (verse 12), can still be called "honest and good." At least this much seems clear: A heart must be *prepared* to receive the gospel in such a way that the receiver will hold fast to God's Word, bear fruit, and remain faithful. It is soil that is not only loose, free of rocks, and without thorns, but it's also ready to receive the seed. Soil that is able to produce a bountiful crop is not raw, untouched land. It has been cultivated. It has been prepared ahead of time to receive the seed.

This parable is not about good seed but about good soil. The emphasis is squarely on the condition and quality of the soil, an image used here to represent a person's heart. In this parable, the seed is *always* good because it's the gospel message, but the soil of human hearts varies greatly. Some hearts have not been prepared for the time of sowing, while others are ready to receive the seed.[1]

As this became clear, I realized that even as I scattered seeds in my child's heart, I needed to pay more attention to soil preparation. An "honest and good heart" is a prepared heart. Those qualities don't save a person, but they prepare a person to be saved. In a child's heart, they are the qualities of godliness instilled by a Christian parent through training and instruction. My real work is not to grow character qualities but to prepare the soil of my child's heart to be ready to receive the seed of God's Word, the gospel. That's when the character growing begins—when the Spirit of God brings Christ's life into my child's heart.

We cultivate the soil of our children's hearts with the language of God's truth, the behaviors of the Christian life, and the reality of God. In essence, we familiarize our children with the ways and words of the kingdom of God so that accepting the gospel, whenever that happens, will be a natural step forward rather than a radical reversal of direction. We are readying their hearts, preparing fertile soil so the gospel can sink deep roots into their lives. When the gospel takes hold, they will be saved from their sins and given a new spirit. Then the Holy Spirit will begin the lifelong process of producing the character of Christ in them.

Parenting is not only the process of sowing plenty of good seeds in hopes that some will take root. It is also, and perhaps mostly, about preparing soil. The task is not to plant enough good seeds to crowd out the world's weedy influences; it's about faithfully preparing the soil of our children's hearts—making it soft and receptive, cultivating it, enriching it with nutrients, watering it, and weeding it. I can throw a zillion seeds of character into my child's heart, but unless his or her heart has been prepared, and until it is changed by Christ, those seeds will be wasted. There must be hoeing if the sowing is to result in growing.

THE RECEPTIVE HEART

As I reflected on the parable, another question came to mind: What exactly is "an honest and good heart" (Luke 8:15) and how do I cultivate it in my children? A literal rendering of the two words Jesus used to describe the prepared heart would be "good and good." The Greek words *kalos* and *agathos* are both used about one hundred times in the New Testament, and they are roughly synonymous. But here Jesus used both words together, so He must have known that His hearers would understand the distinction. In general, *kalos* referred to an aesthetical goodness and *agathos* to an ethical goodness. *Kalos* is the kind of good that is beautiful, noble, and worthy of praise. It describes what is pleasing to God because it reflects the divine ideal. *Agathos* is the kind of good that is useful and beneficial, particularly in a religious sense. It would describe one who does good morally.

Jesus seemed to be saying that the heart that is receptive to God's Word has been prepared and influenced to value and pursue all aspects of goodness. This heart is receptive to the gospel because it recognizes and responds to God's goodness. This heart is still sinful and in need of salvation, just like the heart described as roadside soil, but the good soil is open to God, able to acknowledge the praiseworthiness of the Creator and the benefits of His truth. That quality, like a field prepared for planting, is not there by accident.

I cannot help but think of Timothy when I read Jesus' parable. Timothy was a young man when Paul first preached in Lystra in Asia Minor. Perhaps Timothy responded then to the gospel message and received Christ because, when Paul returned a second time, Timothy followed him. Years later, when Timothy had become one of Paul's most trusted ministers, Paul provided a wonderful confirmation of the parable of the sower as it applies to raising and training children.

In his second letter to Timothy, Paul reminded the young man of his upbringing: "From childhood you have known the sacred writings which are able to give you the wisdom that *leads to salvation* through faith which is in Christ Jesus" (3:15). It was the Word of God, sown by the "sincere faith" of his Jewish grandmother Lois and his mother, Eunice (1:5), that prepared Timothy's heart to respond when he heard the message of salvation. His was surely an "honest and good heart," like the one Jesus described, and the message of salvation found good soil there. Paul affirmed that the good soil was cultivated and prepared in childhood by a godly Jewish mother

(Timothy's father was a Greek). And, from the scriptural accounts of his life, we can see that the seed in Timothy's heart, like the seed sown on good soil, "grew up, and produced a crop a hundred times as great" (Luke 8:8).

After gaining fresh insight into this passage and its application to raising godly children, I began to look for other insights that might put into biblical perspective my parenting and the challenge of disciplining my children. Soon I found a new path to consider, a path that would become a journey of discovery about the nature of childhood, the Bible's teaching on disciplining children, and the role of the Holy Spirit in parenting. The pieces of the puzzle were beginning to fit together.

A NEW PATH FOR PARENTING

If you are like most parents, it's likely that when you hear the word *discipline,* the idea of punishment immediately pops into your mind. That's to be expected, since that is how discipline is commonly understood in the English language. But when Scripture talks about discipline, it conveys a much richer and more relational meaning. If, in your mind, childhood discipline is only an act carried out by a parent upon a child, then you don't have a complete view of biblical discipline.

In the Bible, discipline is always about relationship. In the same way that the whole of Scripture is about God's faithful love relationship with His children, biblical discipline is about your faithful love relationship with your children. Rather than being an isolated act or a burdensome parental duty, discipline is an ongoing relational process. Heartfelt discipline is built on this foundation.

Early in our children's lives, Sally and I started using a word picture to visualize the concept of discipline. We wanted our young children to understand that our discipline was about much more than simply correcting their wrong behavior. It was about helping them to walk on God's "path of life," making sure that they stayed on the path and didn't get tripped up by other influences and messages. We wanted them to see the big picture of God's purpose for discipline and to see themselves in that picture. In using this word picture, Sally and I stumbled upon a foundational biblical teaching: The concept that gives meaning to childhood discipline is the way of life or the path of life, a rich image from the Old Testament.

Throughout the book of Proverbs, for instance, Solomon contrasted the way of the wise with the way of fools. The picture he painted is of two separate paths with opposite destinations: One leads to life, the other to death. God's "way" is a common Old Testament picture of the life of righteousness. In the New Testament, Jesus also developed this idea. He spoke of "the way [that] is narrow that leads to life" (Matthew 7:14), and He called Himself "the way, and the truth, and the life" (John 14:6). He was laying claim to being the fulfillment of a metaphor that Jews had long used: He Himself was God's way of life. Even new Christians, for a time, were called followers of "the Way" (Acts 19:9; 24:14). Though it might not seem so at first glance, this vivid word picture, straight from the Bible, is profoundly applicable to childhood discipline.

To understand the link between discipline and the "way of life," we need to look at the words used for discipline in the Bible. There are two primary words (along with their derivatives): *yasar* in the Old Testament and *paidea* in the New Testament. *Yasar* is translated as discipline, chastisement, and instruction, expressing the idea of correction, but always in the context of growing in godliness and responsiveness to God and walking in His ways. If you study the biblical references to discipline, you'll notice that the normal context for discipline is that of a close, loving, family relationship. We see this in Proverbs 3:11-12: "My son, do not reject the discipline of the LORD or loathe His reproof, for whom the LORD loves He reproves, even as a father corrects the son in whom he delights." Even when Old Testament writers spoke of God's discipline of Israel, they describe punitive measures with the language of family, such as in Deuteronomy

8:5-6: "Thus you are to know in your heart that the LORD your God was disciplining you just as a man disciplines his son. Therefore, you shall keep the commandments of the LORD your God, to walk in His ways and to fear Him." Punishment is sometimes necessary, but instruction is the primary purpose of discipline.

In the New Testament, *paidea* and its derivatives primarily express the idea of discipline and training, and occasionally, instruction. In most cases it communicates the idea of corrective guidance that trains or educates. In some places, the word for reproof or correction is used alongside this word for discipline, indicating that the reproof of Scripture is an integral part of discipline. The suggestion is that biblical discipline can't be separated from biblical reproof: Training in righteousness requires instruction in righteousness. After recounting the influence of Scripture in Timothy's childhood, Paul wrote, "All Scripture is inspired by God and profitable for teaching, for reproof, for correction, for training in righteousness; so that the man of God may be adequate, equipped for every good work" (2 Timothy 3:16-17). That is a good description of the purpose of discipline—to set a person on the way of life. Simply put, biblical discipline is about much more than punishment.

DISCIPLINE AND THE PATH OF LIFE

We are all influenced by the cultural tendency to view discipline only as punishment. To be honest, this narrow view makes things easier on us as parents. If my disciplinary responsibility is fulfilled by a simple act of punishment or correction, then very little else is required of me. But God has issued a much higher calling. Biblical discipline is much more than an act. It is both an ongoing, heart-to-heart relationship and a continuous spiritual interaction with my children. It is far more than simple correction; it is a parent and child walking together along the path of life. That is the Bible's bigger picture.

The Old Testament image of "the way of life" provides the foundation for understanding the simple and direct New Testament admonition to bring up our children in the "training and instruction of the Lord" (Ephesians 6:4, NIV). The strongest Old Testament picture of the path of life as a model for childhood discipline appears in Proverbs 4. Let's walk through this passage together.

In the first nine chapters of Proverbs, Solomon admonishes and implores his teenage sons to follow the wisdom and instruction they have learned from their father and mother. (He sometimes addresses all his sons, and other times just one son.) That wisdom will protect them against the way of evil and guide them in the way of righteousness. Solomon is preparing his sons for adulthood, encouraging them to stay on the "way of wisdom," which is the "path of life."

In Proverbs 4, Solomon recalls his own youth and the encouragement of his father, David, to pursue wisdom. He reminds each son that he has led them along that same path—the path that will bring them life if they heed the instruction they have received and stay off the path that the wicked follow. In a verse rich with imagery and metaphor, Solomon tells them, "But the path of the righteous is like the light of dawn, that shines brighter and brighter until the full day" (verse 18). The wicked will stumble through their lives in darkness, but those who follow God's ways will receive more and more light.

This is the verse that Sally and I shared with our children when we first began telling them about the path of life. We would occasionally take morning walks, starting in the dark and then greeting the dawn. Our children could easily picture Solomon's image as the sky grew lighter and lighter. They could then comprehend the otherwise abstract truth that understanding comes with experience. In terms of Solomon's image, the path of the righteous may begin in a dim light of understanding, but the longer one follows it, the greater one grows in wisdom. In contrast, the wicked walk in darkness not even knowing what it is that makes them stumble because they have no light of understanding (see verse 19).

Solomon counsels each son to keep his father's words "in the midst of your heart" and to "watch over your heart with all diligence, for from it flow the springs of life" (verses 21 and 23). In a final series of admonitions, he tells them how to walk the path of life, with "your eyes [looking] directly ahead" and your gaze "fixed straight in front of you" (verse 25). They are to make sure that their feet stay on the path of life, that they "do not turn to the right nor to the left" and that they "turn [their] foot from evil" (verse 27). This is the same "narrow way" of Jesus' teaching, the narrow way which leads to life (Matthew 7:13-14).

Solomon instructed his sons in what he himself had already discovered: The path of righteousness is the way that brings life. He had led his children on that path from childhood. Now, as young men, the light was still dim, but if they followed the path, they would find more light. They could know this because their father had been there already.

This chapter offers us a picture of the relational process of biblical discipline. When we don't understand this concept, our acts of discipline and correction become only discrete incidents used in an attempt to control a child's behavior. When seen from the perspective of the path of life, however, discipline takes on a much greater significance. It is not just about controlling behavior; it is about directing a child's life toward God.

HEARTFELT DISCIPLINE

We need a picture that, like the vivid image of the path of life, calls to mind the Bible's bigger view of discipline. I have labeled one such picture heartfelt discipline, a phrase that suggests childhood discipline is not a one-sided affair, but a relationship that involves both the heart of the parent and the heart of the child. It's all about heart-to-heart parenting. Both hearts—the parent's and the child's—must be fully engaged in the relationship.

We often aim our disciplinary efforts at the wrong target. We set our sights on stopping and changing a child's wrong behavior, and we miss the real target of shaping and influencing the heart, which is the source of the wrong behavior. If Billy, for example, refuses to share his new toy with his younger brother, Dad can take away the toy to teach Billy that selfishness is wrong. If Billy continues to be selfish, any number of other consequences can be meted out. Through his parent's exercise of power and control, Billy can be made to stop the unwanted behavior. But has his heart been touched? Has the punishment really addressed the selfishness in Billy's heart that generated the selfish behavior?

Selfishness is an internal, spiritual issue, one that needs true biblical discipline, not simply isolated acts of punishment. The concern is not "How can I stop my child's selfish behavior?" but "How can I change the selfish attitude that *causes* my child's selfish behavior?" At this point we enter the realm of our children's hearts and minds, what we usually call the spiritual dimension. This is God's territory, which is not navigated with pat answers, quickie solutions, or "ten things to do when your child tells a lie." This is the realm of relationship, and all the spiritual, emotional, and verbal dynamics that go with it, where simple formulas give way to heart-to-heart relational realities.

To a busy, frustrated parent, applying purely practical solutions to a spiritual problem might seem to "work": It stops a negative behavior. But such practical "solutions" gloss over the real, spiritual problem. Parents can almost always exercise enough power over younger children to gain control over a behavioral problem. But what happens when the parents aren't around to monitor and control the child's wrong behavior? If the root cause hasn't been addressed, then the behavior will continue. If the child develops no internal controls, then external parental controls will have no long-range effect. The real solution is found at the heart level.

This truth brings us back to Solomon's warning in Proverbs 4:23: "Watch over your heart with all diligence, for from it flow the springs of life." The word translated "springs" in this passage is a rare word in Hebrew. Elsewhere in the Old Testament the same word refers to the farthest borders of a piece of land, the extremities or edges. Of the twenty-four times this word is used in the Old Testament, all but one are related to that meaning. Only in this passage is the word translated with the sense of a spring or source. When we bring to this passage the more common use of the word, we get a much different picture of its meaning.

In verse 21, Solomon has told his son to keep all his parental instruction in the "midst of your heart." Why did Solomon want his son to internalize his teachings? Because these teachings, which will give his son wisdom and understanding, will be "life to those who find them" (verse 22). All of Proverbs 4 is a picture of parental discipline, and in verse 23 Solomon tells his son to "watch over" his heart with all "diligence." Both of these words speak of guarding a facility, as a watchman on the wall looks out for the enemy. Hence, Solomon is not telling his son to watch what comes *out* of his heart, but to guard what goes *into* it. He is telling him to train his mind to let in only wisdom and to keep out anything else.

If wisdom and understanding go into his son's heart and mind, then wisdom and understanding will define the borders, or the edges, of his life. Put differently, the borders of his life will be determined by what he allows to fill his heart. Consequently, in the verses following, Solomon warns his son not to practice deceit or to turn his eyes to evil, but to look ahead at the way of wisdom. If he does this, he will enjoy life, real life, as God meant him to know it. Pursue godly wisdom and you will become wise and discerning; pursue things of the world and you will become foolish and naive.

These verses from Proverbs give us a useful paradigm that can correct a common, but misguided, approach to parenting and discipline. Let's say that there are two kinds of parents: those who watch over what comes *out of* their child's heart and mind, and those who watch over what goes *into* their child's heart and mind. The first group is vigilant to restrain their child's sin (what comes out of the child's heart). They carefully watch over their child's words and actions so as to catch the sin as soon as it appears. When the child sins, there is an immediate and usually negative response from the parents. Punishment (the negative response) is administered to convince the child that the enjoyment of sin pales in comparison to the distasteful consequences of the wrong behavior.

While there is nothing wrong with negative discipline, such as punishment, the real issue is the parents' attitude toward their child. If parents are primarily looking out for sin, they can too easily view their child as an adversary who is trying to get away with bad words and behaviors. This perspective puts parents in the role of sin-squad police, watching for and punishing violations of the law. You've seen these parents before—strict, controlling, often demanding, and always alert to their child's every move. It's difficult, if not impossible, to cultivate a heart-to-heart relationship under those conditions.

But God didn't call us to be sin police; He desires us to be wise and loving parents. He wants us to watch over what is going *into* our children's hearts and to see how those things are shaping the borders of their lives. God asks us parents to be life-giving influences, the ones who give the words of life to our children. Of course, we must still restrain our children's sin. But how we perceive ourselves in our relationship with our children will make all the difference in their lives. We can either be an adversary or an advocate. To walk with our children on the path of life, we need to be the latter.

So rather than obsessing over what comes out of a child's heart, an advocate parent focuses on what goes into his or her heart. Such parenting is all about cultivating "good soil" that will receive the truth of the gospel. The parents' role is to prepare a child's heart to receive the seed of the Word of God that will "lead to salvation." That is the seed that will produce the fruit of Christian character, the actual life of Christ in a child's heart. The training and instruction that parents provide their children is the process of giving them the words and ways of the Christian life so that, like Timothy, when they are saved, they will continue on the path they're already walking on.

Heartfelt discipline is all about becoming an advocate for your children as you exercise your biblical responsibility to discipline them. It's about looking at your children through a new biblical lens. It's about understanding the spiritual dimension of your child's nature so that you can better connect with his or her heart. It's about pursuing the larger biblical picture of discipline, seeing yourself as a godly guide for your children along the path of life.

WALKING ON THE PATH OF LIFE

Childhood is a God-ordained time of life that He has designed with a specific purpose. It is a formative time managed by loving parents. Childhood, as I've stated earlier, is to be characterized by parents and children who are walking together on the path of life.

You are a godly guide, directing your children in wisdom and righteousness. You are training and instructing them about how to walk this path in order to find life as God intended it to be. You are also warning them about the dangers that would lead them away from the path and correcting them when they stray from the path. This full, biblical picture of discipline reflects an ongoing heart-to-heart relationship in which you are patiently and lovingly guiding your child.

When your children leave childhood and step into young adulthood, they will begin to walk the path on their own. If you prepared the soil of their hearts well, the gospel will find root there, and the Spirit will turn them toward Christ. They will begin to follow God on their own, and they will continue to grow in the character of Christ. Childhood discipline is a process, not a formula, a list of rules, or a set of laws. Childhood discipline is about relationship and instruction, about parents seeking God's wisdom, walking in the power of the Holy Spirit, and trusting God.

Scripture offers no step-by-step formula that guarantees success. Rather than outlining a specific method, God provides the Holy Spirit, who frees us from man-made laws to follow the Law of God that He writes on our hearts. Our confidence in parenting comes from walking in the power of the Holy Spirit and learning how to discipline our children by faith; our confidence does not come from how well we follow rules. This approach is far from easy, however, since our natural inclination is to look for specific guidelines and surefire keys to success. Because disciplining children is a demanding and confusing process, we seek a formula that works every time, with every child, in every instance.

The apostle John wrote in his last letter, "I have no greater joy than this, to hear of my children walking in the truth" (3 John 4). John's "children" are grown-up believers, of course, but the image he draws upon is that of a father thinking of his own young children. What Christian father would not identify with John's desire? It's my own greatest desire to know the joy of seeing my precious children walking in God's truth, confidently progressing along God's path of life. This book is all about finding that joy in an unlikely place: through disciplining our children in this biblical way.

In the chapters that follow, we'll look more closely at the road signs that point us in a new direction for biblical discipline. It will be a journey of discovery for some, a journey of confirmation for others, but a rewarding journey for all. Before we examine the biblical concept of discipline, though, let's take a closer look at what God had in mind when He designed the time of life we call childhood.

CHAPTER 2

THE HEART
OF CHILDHOOD

Seeing Your Child Through God's Eyes

Train up a child in the way he should go,
Even when he is old he will not depart from it.

PROVERBS 22:6

You've met her at church or in your neighborhood. Maybe you *are* her. Let's call her Ellen. She has two delightful school-age children. She loves being a mother and is devoted to raising godly children. But lately the calling of Christian parenthood has become a daily challenge. It's harder and harder for Ellen to find joy amid all the frustrating attempts to discipline.

Her children are energetic, bright, and inquisitive, yet very different from each other. Her older child, a girl, is the compliant type—always wanting to please her parents and usually doing what is asked. Yet Ellen wonders if she is really reaching her child's heart. Is her daughter's cooperative nature evidence of a heart turned toward God or simply her innate temperament?

Ellen's younger child, a boy, is full of spit and energy. He is respectful to his parents most of the time, but he clearly has a mind of his own and often chooses his own path. His sister is quick to do the dishes when asked, but when it's her brother's turn, he's quick to ask, "Why do *I* have to?" He naturally attracts the most attention when it comes to discipline.

Ellen has read all the popular discipline manuals and has tried everything with her son. Nothing—not scoldings, loss of privileges, or time-outs—seems to slow him down. Spankings might work for a brief moment, but thirty minutes later he seems to have forgotten the reason for the spanking. Most of what Ellen has read suggests that if Christian parents fail to spank their children, they are somehow disobeying God's requirements. She has continued the spankings, but they never produce the long-lasting results that the experts promise. And what's worse, spanking makes Ellen feel distant from her son, as though she has become a police officer—making arrests and dishing out punishment—rather than being the loving mommy she really wants to be.

While her son seems to shrug off the spankings, Ellen wonders why she never needs to spank her daughter, who automatically knows how to win her mother's favor. Even so, Ellen has noticed that her daughter can be self-righteous and judgmental toward others. She doesn't feel that such an attitude calls for a spanking, but she's uncertain how to reach her daughter's heart and what the best form of discipline is to address the bad attitude. Ellen's son gets spanked because he's quick to express his attitudes, but her daughter avoids spankings by being smart enough to keep quiet. It doesn't seem to Ellen that biblically based discipline should discriminate on the basis of a child's candor.

If spanking has such strong scriptural endorsement, why isn't it working in Ellen's family? She feels that her disciplinary methods are missing something important, but she can't put her finger on it. She senses that there's a better way to reach her children's hearts and point them to God. She wants to love them equally and consistently, and she wants to be fair in her discipline. Most important, how can she relate to her son and daughter in a way that accurately reflects what God says about children and discipline?

Frustrated, Ellen keeps doing what she's been doing and pushes the nagging questions to the back of her mind. She silently recites what she believes is the biblical promise that a child raised in a Christian home will not depart from those values when he is older, but that doesn't help her much. She loves her children but can't escape the feeling that her joy in being a mother is slipping away.

THE DISCIPLINE DILEMMA

There is perhaps no verse of Scripture quoted more frequently by Christian parents than Solomon's pithy little statement, "Train up a child in the way he should go, even when he is old he will not depart from it" (Proverbs 22:6). It is a succinct statement of a parent's mission, an Old Testament principle gilded with the promise that godly discipline will prevail even if it takes awhile. Chances are you know this verse by heart, or you have it on a plaque hanging on your child's bedroom wall, or you have underlined it in your Bible.

All of those are true for me. Like many other parents, especially when my children were very young, I have turned to this verse more times than I can remember. For example, when my firstborn, Sarah, was about four years old, I was standing in the checkout line with her at the grocery store. As we waited, she grabbed one of the colorful candies placed right at her eye level. I told her no, and I put the candy back, whereupon Sarah took a different candy from the display. This pattern repeated itself, and each time she held up the candy and asked me to buy it for her.

This was too much. I swatted her lightly on the back of the leg and spoke to her in a firm voice. I felt I was obeying God's command to "train up a child in the way he should go." An inner voice was telling me to punish even Sarah's minor infractions so she would know that her dad was in control. If I had known then what I know now, I would have handled the situation entirely differently. I would have picked her up (removing her from the temptation of the candy display), asked her what her favorite thing was in our shopping cart, and then had her help place the grocery items on the conveyor belt. But I was a new parent then, and I lacked wisdom. At that time my attitudes toward discipline had more to do with punishment and asserting control than with training my child and guiding her toward God. It was all about controlling my daughter's misbehavior, not about reaching her little heart.

At that moment, and in many other similar situations, I needed to be reminded of just what it was that God wanted me to do. During that challenging and mysterious season of parenting, when it seemed as though each year found me considering a new discipline strategy, the passage in Proverbs became a kind of biblical tonic for me. When yet another approach proved ineffective or unrealistic and I would wonder what impact, if any, all my "training" was having, I could at least rest in the shaky assurance that it would all matter someday when my children were grown.

It is during the childhood years, roughly the time between toddlerhood and teenhood, that parental confidence faces its toughest tests. This was true for me, anyway. There's no doubt that raising young children is a delightful time of life filled with blossoming personality, disarming innocence, enthusiastic discovery, and childish mirth that keep parents young at heart. Those are exciting and fulfilling years of watching a new person emerge from what started out as a helpless baby. But as a unique person emerges, so does the sin nature. That newly discovered will tests a parent's resolve and confidence.

As much as I enjoyed those years with my precious children, I also struggled to find the most effective and most biblical way to exercise my parental authority. I could get a fairly good handle on my role as a father and parent, but how to discipline my young children was always a hands-on issue (double entendre intended). Not a day seemed to go by that didn't require Sally and me to deal with the issues of discipline—what was too much, what was not enough, and what wasn't worth bothering with. That's when Proverbs 22:6 became my release valve. Whatever I did about discipline, I fell back on the promise of that passage to cover my mistakes.

Things change, though. Today, as a fiftyish father of four, I've seen two children, first a girl and then a boy, pass through childhood into young adulthood. I have a third, a near-teen boy, with one foot firmly planted in childhood and the other inching across the line into male adolescence. Then I have a fourth child basking in the glory of girlish, six-year-old childhood. So not only have I been there and done that, but I've gone back for more. My little girl, Joy, will have the benefit of being raised by seasoned parents who have less to prove and more to approve after the successes and failures learned at the expense of the older siblings.

But here's where I have to get even more honest. After nearly eighteen years of parenting, Proverbs 22:6 no longer assuages my feelings of inadequacy. It's no longer a tonic to ward off my uncertainty and confusion about discipline. In fact, I've come to believe that this passage doesn't address the childhood years at all. After a decade of studying what God has to say about children, discipline, and parenting, I've reached this conclusion: God has very little to say directly about childhood discipline or, for that matter, about the period of life we call childhood.

Please don't stop reading just yet. There is much to learn about children from God's Word, including tremendous insights into discipline. Yet what we know about childhood from God's perspective is mostly anecdotal, not instructional. In other words, Scripture contains many stories in which children play a role, but there are very few direct commands for parents about raising children. God has not provided enough specific teaching for us to construct a theology of childhood or a doctrine of discipline. Nonetheless, there are clear insights, principles, and perspectives throughout Scripture that teach us much about children. Put them all together and the role of the parent in God's design for childhood pops out like the hidden image in a 3-D Magic Eye picture. You just have to look long enough to see the image emerge from the clutter of clashing views.

The verse that seems to promise a good outcome, Proverbs 22:6, is itself a good example. At first glance, it appears to guarantee the results we seek: Be a diligent parent and you won't be disappointed. Look at it longer and deeper though, and a different picture begins to emerge. In chapter 3, we'll look under the surface of this verse and enter into a paradigm-shifting discussion of just who the child is. And that, in turn, will lead to a defining discussion of what childhood discipline is from a biblical perspective.

For now, though, it's helpful to fashion a picture of childhood from the many small snapshots we get in the Bible. Despite the paucity of specific "thus saith the Lord" references, we can still learn much about children from God's Word. But before we talk about discipline, let's get a handle on the period of life we know as childhood. What is it that God is most concerned about when He gives us children to raise?

THE HEART OF CHILDHOOD

When we read 1 Corinthians, we can see that Paul viewed childhood as a special and specific time of life: "When I was a child, I used to speak like a child, think like a child, reason like a child; when I became a man, I did away with childish things" (13:11). Paul recognized that childhood is a period of development toward maturity, one through which we all must pass. There are childish ways of speaking, thinking, and reasoning that we must leave behind to move into adulthood. This idea is echoed in Ephesians, when Paul wrote that we are to attain to the goal of becoming a "mature man" and that "we are no longer to be children" (4:13-14).

Before we consider the question of childhood discipline, we need first to get a better grasp not only of the nature of childhood, but also of what God thinks about this period of life. I've identified four general truths regarding the biblical view of childhood that lay a foundation for this book's discussion of discipline. The four core truths are:

1. Childhood is a divinely designed stage of life.
2. A child's heart is divinely open to parental influence.
3. A child's mind is divinely prepared for believing in God.
4. A child's soul is divinely protected by the heavenly Father.

Biblical insights about childhood are just as often implicit as they are explicit, so I'll avoid being dogmatic. These four truths are my attempt to define some of the characteristics of the time of life we call childhood, the period up to about age twelve or thirteen.

The Special Nature of Childhood

Are the years of early childhood merely a preformative time that leads eventually to "real" personhood? Is it a transitional period that bridges a gap but doesn't really add anything substantive to becoming an adult? Or is it a divinely designed stage of life and thus imbued with eternal purpose and meaning? The Bible teaches that God built special meaning and purpose into the years of early childhood. Discovering the nature of childhood is therefore the first step to fully understanding God's plan for childhood discipline.

The accepted view of childhood has varied dramatically throughout time. Cultural and historical forces have shaped whether children are disdained, enjoyed, ignored, used, or allowed to run wild. One current notion of childhood views it as a magical time during which certain markers of personhood begin to emerge, but the child is somehow a "pre-person"—incomplete, innocent, and naive. According to this view, the best thing parents can do is allow their child to experience childhood in all its mystical, Disneyfied wonder. Soon enough, the argument goes, that child will emerge from this protected time of life as a teenager, and then everything changes.

You may identify with that view or some other one, but such cultural notions of childhood can get in the way of our search for the biblical view. Until we understand what God had in mind when He included childhood in the plan for human development, we're handicapped in our ability to understand our children. And if we don't understand them, how can we ever be confident about how to discipline them effectively?

Nowhere does Scripture suggest that God created childhood as a kind of parenthesis, a period of developmental stasis preceding puberty. Rather, childhood can be seen in Scripture as a specific time of life that is both necessary and preparatory for the stage that follows. Childhood seems to be part of a three-stage sequence of human development: childhood…young adult…adult. Each stage moves with nearly seamless continuity into the next, each a part of the others and yet distinct from the others.

In John's first letter, the apostle addressed three groups: fathers, young men, and children (see 2:13-14). I realize that John used "little children" to refer to followers of Jesus who, to the ninety-year-old John, must have seemed like little children. However, it seems likely that he was also reflecting a use, or pattern, of words that would have been familiar to his readers. Although the Hebrew words used in the Old Testament are not as precise as the Greek words of the New Testament, we also see references elsewhere in Scripture to similar life-stage delineations. Most of us, if asked to describe the stages of life in the simplest sense, would narrow it down to childhood, youth (or adolescence), and adulthood. And that's what we find fairly consistently throughout Scripture.

Contrast those three stages with our culture's breakdown of life development. Factoring in our longer lifespans, twelve-plus years of age-graded schooling, and a consumer culture steeped in demographics and market segmentation, the resulting sequence of life stages is harder to follow: infancy, toddlerhood, preschool, childhood, preteen, teenager, young adult, young married, adult, empty nester, senior. Those all sound very plausible to our culture-tuned ears, and you can find references in the Scriptures to the very young (usually "infants") and the very old (usually "elders"). However, nowhere do I find Scripture suggesting the amount of fragmentation between those ends of the age spectrum that our culture suggests.

In God's developmental design, one begins life in childhood and then at age twelve or thirteen becomes a young adult. And, in the same way that childhood is preparatory for young adulthood, young adulthood is the preparatory stage for full adulthood, which usually includes the expectation of being a spouse and parent. Each of the three stages is distinct, with a specific purpose. Until we can grasp the nature and significance of childhood as distinct from young adulthood, we can't understand the role of discipline in the life of a young child.

The Special Openness of a Child's Heart

B. F. Skinner, the twentieth-century social scientist who popularized the school of psychology called behaviorism, argued that all human behavior is conditioned. In other words, each of us comes into the world as a tabula rasa, an empty slate, and who we are is defined by what circumstances, experiences, and other stimuli write on the tablet of our otherwise empty minds. Skinner would claim that, if given a newborn, he could shape and mold that child into whatever kind of person he wanted simply by controlling the positive and negative stimuli.

You might be thinking that some of that sounds reasonable, even biblical. Aren't parents—especially *Christian* parents—supposed to shape and mold the lives of their babies? Isn't that what character training is all about? Hang onto those questions because we'll explore that idea more in chapter 4. For now, though, consider the notion of the blank slate or, to use a metaphor more suitable to our technological age, the empty hard drive. Does a child enter the world with no prior programming, just an unformatted blank disk filled with nothing but magnetic zeros?

The Bible assumes that a child comes into life divinely open to the influence of his or her parents and teaches that, before birth, the slate is already written upon. To be specific, the child bears the marks of the Creator God on his or her soul—the imago dei, the image of God. As a parent, you know intuitively that your child is not a blank disk. Rather, your child's mind is preformatted and already loaded with an infinitely complex program, ready-to-run out of the box, and just waiting for your instructions. It's not your responsibility to program your child, but rather to run the program that God has already put there.

If you question this view, think about all the things babies know without being taught. Children don't need to be taught how to learn to speak. The capacity for learning a language is already programmed into their mental and physiological abilities. In the same way, children are prewired to know how to learn to read. Though we guide them in learning to read in a particular language, they already possess the inherent ability to associate symbols, sounds, and meaning. Along with the ability to speak and to read, there is a hunger for knowledge that you didn't put there, along with nascent curiosity, reasoning, and creativity. These are marks of the image of God, placed within every person by their Creator (see Genesis 1:26-27).

But the programming doesn't end with distinctive human traits and abilities, such as language learning and higher-level thinking. God has also programmed into every child's being a readiness and openness to being spiritually influenced by his or her parents. We see this in the *shema,* to Jews one of the most important Old Testament passages: "Hear, O Israel! The LORD is our God, the LORD is one! And you shall love the LORD your God with all your heart and with all your soul and with all your might. These words, which I am commanding you today, shall be on your heart. You shall teach them diligently to your sons and shall talk of them when you sit in your house and when you walk by the way and when you lie down and when you rise up.... You shall write them on the doorposts of your house and on your gates" (Deuteronomy 6:4-9). This passage, still repeated daily by pious Jews, assumes that children are open to the spiritual influence of their parents. Moses, speaking to the families of Israel gathered on the plains of Moab just before they entered the Promised Land, made it clear that God's commandments were first to be on the parents' hearts and then passed on to the children. He gave parents the model for passing on righteousness from one generation to the next. In that model, there is no place or time that parents are *not* to teach God's commandments diligently to their children. It is assumed that children are open and ready for this parental nurture and influence.

Psalm 78 also affirms the truth that a child's heart is prepared by God to be influenced by his or her parents: "For He established a testimony in Jacob and appointed a law in Israel, which He commanded our fathers that they should teach them to their children" (verse 5). This process of passing faith from one generation to the next, which looks back to the *shema,* is a natural process ordained by God that will involve "even the children yet to be born, that they may arise and tell…their children" to trust God, to remember His faithfulness, and to obey His commandments (verses 6-7). God has prepared the hearts of our children to respond to our influence.

In the New Testament, the apostle Paul assumed this openness to parental influence when he commanded fathers not to frustrate their children but rather to "bring them up in the discipline and instruction of the Lord" (Ephesians 6:4). The implication is that children are "provoked to anger," or frustrated, when parents fail to fulfill God's calling to spiritually influence them.

Many other Scriptures reinforce the truth that children come preprogrammed with a sensitivity and an openness to their parents. Underlying so many scriptural references to childhood is the assumption that, just as their earthly fathers will ready them for future stages of growth, their heavenly Father has already prepared them for growth during childhood.

The Special Preparation of a Child's Mind

Have you ever seen a man, a woman, and two or three children in a crowd and known without question that they are a family? There is a distinct look that shouts to the world, "We're related, and there's no denying it!" People have commented to Sally and me that our children bear marks that clearly identify them as Clarksons. Some strong genes have carried forward a number of common physical characteristics (although it took until child number four to get my brown-eyed genes into the mix). But the "Clarkson look" also means that our children exhibit nonphysical traits, such as certain convictions, habits, mannerisms, and beliefs that are common to the

Clarkson tribe. And all of those characteristics were passed on to them by their parents.

Just so, the "image of God" is roughly in view when we consider what we've been given from our heavenly Father. When God created humanity in Genesis 1:26-27, He created both man and woman after His own "likeness" and "in His own image, in the image of God." Adam and Eve resembled, in some way, the Creator God. We're never told exactly what it means to bear the image of God, but it would seem from the Genesis account to have to do with relationship, intellect, creativity, fruitfulness, and stewardship (see Genesis 1:28-30).

The quality of our humanness, that which makes us persons and not animals, is tied directly to the image of God within us. Later, in Genesis 5:1-2, God reiterated His original stamp on man and woman, using the same words found in the creation account. But then we read, referring to Adam's son Seth, that Adam "became the father of a son in his own likeness, according to his image" (verse 3). In other words, the nonphysical image of God is passed on from parent to child through the physical image of the parent.

There is a spiritual reality already present in your child from the moment of conception that comes *from* God, but it comes *through* you. In Psalm 139:13 David marveled, "For You formed my inward parts; You wove me in my mother's womb."

The term *inward parts* is a Hebrew term for the mind and heart. Clearly, God was at work within David before his birth, shaping and forming the very core of his personhood. Later, David's son Solomon said about all mankind that God "has also set eternity in their heart" (Ecclesiastes 3:11), and Paul taught that everybody has the "work of the Law written in their hearts" (Romans 2:15). Your children come into this world both with a longing for eternity that will drive them to seek out the meaning and purpose of life, as well as an innate, though immature, sense of right and wrong that will eventually bring them to accountability before the God of eternity.

Perhaps the strongest voice in Scripture for the reality of a spiritual nature in children is that of Jesus Himself. When His disciples wanted to know, "Who then is greatest in the kingdom of heaven?" Jesus called over a young child, probably a boy, to join them (Matthew 18:1-2). The disciples, of course, wanted names: Which of them would be most honored in what they thought would be the restored kingdom of Israel with Jesus on the throne? Jesus, though, gave His disciples an example instead: Whoever of them "humbles himself as this child," who responded immediately to the Savior's call, would be the greatest in the kingdom of heaven (18:2-4). Surely the disciples were somewhat offended by Jesus' comparing them to a child, who would have no rights under Jewish law. Later, the disciples' prideful hearts would be further shamed when they refused access to some children who had been brought to Jesus for His blessing. Jesus quickly rebuked the disciples for hindering the little ones and said, to their amazement I'm sure, "The kingdom of heaven belongs to such as these" (19:14). This was the answer to their earlier unanswered question—although certainly not the answer the disciples were hoping for!

Jesus even warned His disciples that anyone who causes "one of these little ones who believe in Me to stumble" (NIV: "to sin"), will definitely not want to have to explain himself to God at the Judgment (Matthew 18:5-6). Jesus was rebuking His disciples' attitude toward children, but don't trip over some important words here. Jesus was talking about very little children (*paidion,* up to about seven years old), and He described them as those "who believe in Me." In those words, Jesus acknowledges the spiritual nature of even young children. They can believe in Him! Their faith is valid. It's not a mature faith, to be sure, but there is a nascent faith in a child, devoid of pride and unhindered by self-promotion, that Jesus recognized and even commended. It's the kind of faith Jesus wants to see in His adult followers. When He said that these children "believe," He used the same word used throughout the New Testament to describe saving faith (*pisteuo*). It's an innocent faith, and the Savior affirms it.

You know that your child is divinely prepared to believe in God. A child's heart is open not only to parental influence, but also to truth about God. Your child is ready to hear and respond to the reality of the living God. He won't be able to understand all the abstract truths about the nature of God, the reality of sin, and our need for salvation; but he can believe in what he cannot yet see. Jesus told the doubtful Thomas, who needed physical proof of Christ's resurrection, "Because you have seen Me, have you believed? Blessed are they who did not see, and yet believed" (John 20:29). It is your responsibility as a parent to cultivate that belief. Just as your child's heart bears the image of God because of you, your child will also believe in the God who put it there because of you.

The Special Protection of a Child's Soul

The first three aspects of childhood—the special nature of childhood, the special openness of a child's heart, and the special preparation of a child's mind—raise a big question, though: What about sin? Every parent wonders what would happen to her young children if they should die unexpectedly. Would their inherited sin nature leave God no choice but to condemn them to hell? And what about children with mental handicaps?

Several years ago I was pastor of a small church we had planted. One dear family that lived near us had eight children, one of them a three-year-old boy with Down syndrome. In the middle of a winter night, we received a frantic call that something was wrong with their little boy. By the time we reached the house, the paramedics were carrying the limp little body to the waiting ambulance. They were taking him to the hospital even though he was surely already dead from an undetected heart condition. I went to the hospital with his father and did my best to be a comfort and support. I couldn't help wondering what I would do and think if this boy were my own child. But I also found myself wondering what I, as a pastor, could say to assure my friend that God loved his son and would welcome him into eternity. I wondered what Scripture I could quote to speak to the eternal fate of a young boy with a mental handicap.

Even if your own child has never suffered life-threatening injuries or illness, you still wonder "what if?" What if he chases a ball into the street and is hit by a car? Will he spend eternity with God? What is saving faith, or belief, for a little child, and when and how should I encourage it? Is there an "age of accountability" and if there is, when does it begin? Is my young child innocent in God's eyes, or guilty and condemned?

If you have searched the Scriptures looking for answers to these questions, you have discovered that clear answers are hard to find. There are multiple shades of gray on this issue, and regardless of how hard we try to add contrast, they can't be turned into black and white. It's not lazy or irresponsible to say that God's answer to these questions is part of what Paul called the "mystery of the gospel" (Ephesians 6:18-20). God simply has not made this issue clear, and we should guard against trying to make Scripture say more than it really says. However, what you believe about your child's soul will directly influence what you believe about childhood discipline.

THE QUESTION OF MORAL ACCOUNTABILITY

I won't try to fully defend a doctrine of childhood innocence or define childhood culpability in the following few paragraphs. However, there are some truths we can know for sure from Scripture, and there are some reasonable conclusions we can draw. Consider the thoughts that follow as a starting place for your own study of this issue.

What Scripture Says

First, it's clear from Scripture that every child is born with a sin nature. Paul strongly asserted in Romans 5:12-19 that sin and death came to "all men," a term used for all people as distinct from animals, because of

Adam's disobedience. Therefore, in the same way that we pass on the image of God to our children, we also pass on a sin nature. Your child doesn't become a sinner only when he begins to knowingly sin; rather, he sins because he is, from conception, a sinner. The sin nature, in addition to separating us from God, has also distorted the image of God within each of us, which is why the best we can ever do on our own is but a dim, imperfect reflection of God's original intention for us.

Not all is lost because of sin, though. Because your child carries the image of God, he can still do relative good in an earthly sense—he can learn to obey, show love and tenderness, say kind things, and even take initiative to be responsible without your asking (really!). However, he can do no good in God's eyes apart from Christ. The relative good a child does will not merit or earn God's approval, "for all have sinned and fall short of the glory of God" (Romans 3:23). Apart from Christ, even our best efforts are like "a filthy garment" in God's eyes (Isaiah 64:6). The Jews mistakenly thought keeping the Law of Moses would make them acceptable to God, but Paul said that God gave the Law in order to reveal sin so His grace could prevail, not to solve the problem of sin (see Romans 5:18-21).

Second, though, I also know from Scripture that God's ultimate desire for your child is that he or she receive God's grace and come to know Him. "For all have sinned" is followed by this truth: "being justified as a gift by His grace through the redemption which is in Christ Jesus" (Romans 3:24). God has provided the solution for sin: redemption. With the blood of Christ, He has paid the price that will set us free from our slavery to sin. Because "God so loved the world," He gave His only Son, Jesus, that "whoever believes in Him shall not perish, but have eternal life" (John 3:16). That is the grace of God, and it's there for your child. Peter said that God "is patient toward you, not wishing for *any* to perish but for *all* to come to repentance" (2 Peter 3:9). God's desire that everyone know His grace holds true for your children. God loves them and wants them to become His children.

Third, Scripture also indicates that there is a point when a person becomes aware of his or her sinful condition. In Romans 7, Paul flashed back to a time when he was "once alive apart from the Law." But, he said, "when the commandment [that is, the Law] came, sin became alive and I died" (verse 9). This is very likely a reference to his own bar mitzvah at age thirteen, when he accepted the responsibility as a young man to live under the Law (young children were not considered accountable to the Law). The Law revealed Paul's sin, but could not deal with it; the Law made him more acutely aware of his sin, but provided no way for him to overcome it. Desperate for a Savior, Paul recalled the cry of his soul, "Wretched man that I am! Who will set me free from the body of this death?" (verse 24). The answer to his question is in Romans 8, Paul's declaration of the freedom he found in Christ. Your child will reach a similar point in his own life, a time when the reality of sin comes crashing in on his soul. He will no longer find his faith identity in you, and he will begin to "own" his own relationship with Christ. At this point he must choose what to do with Jesus Christ on his own; at this point he will pass from childhood into young adulthood.

Fourth, some scriptures indicate that there is a time when a child becomes aware of right and wrong, and only then does the child become morally accountable to God. When Israel was about to cross the Jordan and enter the Promised Land, Moses recounted why an entire generation was judged because of its unfaithfulness and rebellion forty years earlier. With the exception of the faithful two, Caleb and Joshua, all of the adult generation that had come out of Egypt had died in the wilderness. Moses said, "Moreover, your little ones who you said would become a prey, and your sons, who this day have no knowledge of good or evil, shall enter there, and I will give it to them and they shall possess it" (Deuteronomy 1:39).

The children of those adults escaped the judgment because they had "no knowledge of good or evil." One of the terms for "child" used in this passage, *taph,* is derived from a Hebrew word that means "to take small steps," indicating a young child. This passage can't be used to establish sinless innocence, but it does indicate that there is a time when young children are not yet accountable, or culpable, for their sin. Isaiah suggested the same idea in his prophecy about Immanuel: "…at the time He knows enough to refuse evil and choose good" (Isaiah 7:15). From a different perspective, King David was confident that he would once again see his infant child who had died, even though the child was taken by God because of David's own sin with Bathsheba (see 2 Samuel 12:21-23).

Other scriptures offer indirect insights. Luke alone records the time when Jesus, at twelve years of age, impressed the priests at the temple and reminded His parents that it was time for Him to be about His Father's business (see 2:49, KJV). Luke notes that Jesus "continued in subjection" to His parents and "kept increasing" from that point on "in wisdom and stature, and in favor with God and men" (2:51-52). Perhaps the Holy Spirit inspired Luke to include this event to show that there is a point in life when a child moves out of moral neutrality and into his own accountability before God.

It is also worth noting, even though arguments from silence are less persuasive, that nowhere in Scripture does God: (1) condemn the condition of childhood, (2) indicate that all children are rebellious sinners, or (3) suggest that children are under judgment because of their own sin. To the contrary, the language regarding childhood, whether from God or others, is generally positive.[1] There are scattered references to "capricious" and "stupid" children, but generally children are considered innocent and vulnerable, in need of protection. The condition of childhood is often used as a positive example: Jesus pointed to young children as examples of those who could inherit the kingdom of God (see Matthew 18:3), used a young boy's meal to feed five thousand people (see John 6:1-14), and welcomed children as He ministered (see Matthew 19:13-15). He looked at children much differently than did the Pharisees, who generally disdained them.

What We Can Say

What can we conclude about the state of a child's soul? Here's what makes biblical sense to me. First, Scripture nowhere defines a specific "age of accountability." The focus of Scripture is not to establish an age, as in creating a legal point in time; rather, Scripture defines the nature and need of the "accountability." In other words, the age of accountability will vary from child to child, but there does seem to be a point when a child moves out of childhood innocence and into a new state of accountability to God. If it's not a specific age, then what defines that shift?

I believe the shift happens when a child comes into a full awareness of his own sinful nature and the separation that it brings between him and the holy Creator God, to whom he is now accountable. Now the child must decide what to do about that sin that separates him from God. If he sees it, abhors it, and rejects it, he will begin to move toward God for the solution that is found only in Christ (see Romans 7:24-25). If he sees it, ignores it, and gives in to it, he will carry the full weight of the guilt of Adam's sin. If he continues on that path, he will harden his heart and turn further from God. In either case, the sin was there all along, but now the child is accountable for it. This process of awareness and responsibility marks the beginning of young adulthood.

It also makes sense that, though my child may be technically guilty before God because of her sin nature, she may be innocent before God in regard to the Law. That innocence is not the absence of sin; rather, it is the postponement of culpability. When the Law (that is, the mature understanding of right from wrong) has the effect, in Paul's words, of causing sin to "spring to life," that is when a child becomes fully guilty before God (see Romans 7:7-13). Until then, it would seem that a child's family is to be her moral incubator, and parents, the protectors and nurturers of the formative life (see 2 Timothy 3:15), indicating that the real accountability for a child during those years lies with the parents.

Finally, I can trust in the nature and character of God. My finite need for certainty and precision about the condition of my child's soul does not trump God's divine reasons, whatever they may be, for leaving this issue undefined.[2] But I know that God is just and merciful, full of grace, faithful, kind, and abounding in lovingkindness. And I know that He has a special place in His heart and in His eternal plan for children. So I can rest knowing the character of God.

By way of contrast, it makes no biblical sense to assert that infants and children, who by God's design are not yet capable of making morally informed decisions, could die in their sins and be condemned to hell. It makes no biblical sense that talking my children into "praying the sinner's prayer"—to confess their sin and accept Christ as their Savior—will necessarily save them. If they do so to please me rather than God, or because they feel coerced or expected to pray the prayer, then the prayer is sweet, but it is not likely a sinner's prayer of repentance and a true plea for mercy and forgiveness. It's better to prepare the soil of our children's hearts by teaching them to love, honor, and obey God and by filling their lives with His truth. When the time is right, the seed of the gospel will find good soil and lead our children to salvation.

God's grace extends in a special way to young children. My anxious concerns about the state of my child's soul must, in some way, be balanced by my understanding of what God is like. Very little is said in Scripture about my child's soul that would assuage my parental fears. However, much is said in Scripture about God's nature and character that should give me reason to trust Him with my children. In the end, it's my responsibility to "bring them up in the training and instruction of the Lord" (Ephesians 6:4, NIV), and then to entrust their souls to the care of my loving and merciful God during the mysterious years of childhood.

The Bible gives us no special formula or words or ritual to employ before our children come into their own accountable relationship with

God. There is only this call: that we love our children and trust them to our God who loves children. That *should* be enough, but for many of us it's not. So let's look at one of the most popular, and most misunderstood, methods of disciplining children: the use of "the rod."

CHAPTER 3

SPARING THE ROD...

Without Spoiling the Child

He who withholds his rod hates his son,
But he who loves him disciplines him diligently.

PROVERBS 13:24

S pare the rod, spoil the child." If you conducted a quick poll, you'd likely find more people attributing this proverb to Benjamin Franklin than to its actual source, King Solomon. But Christian parents who have done much reading on child rearing, and especially on discipline, know the adage comes straight out of the Old Testament.[1]

Beginning in the 1950s, with the influence of Dr. Benjamin Spock, parents chose a hands-off approach to child rearing. Children were allowed to experiment with things and freely explore their surroundings in the name of self-expression. Parents would stand back and observe, intervening only if the child's life were in danger. But what about the child's spirit? Many experts track the cultural narcissism of later decades to the shift in discipline approaches that began in the fifties. Parents spoiled their children, and, as a society, we've been paying for it ever since.

In response to the extreme latitude that was being granted to children, a new emphasis was later championed by Christian parenting experts. Many advocated a return to the biblical teaching of "the rod." A parent who took an extreme hands-off approach to discipline didn't truly love his child, they argued. Instead, appropriate parental love must include the discipline of the rod in certain matters of child rearing. It seemed clear, moreover, that God required nothing less from Christian parents. Bolstering that argument are verses such as, "He who withholds his rod hates his son, but he who loves him disciplines him diligently" (Proverbs 13:24).

Even if you don't consider a passage such as Proverbs 13:24 to be God's mandated formula for childhood discipline, you've had to decide what to do with this verse and others like it. Every dad who considers himself a strict disciplinarian is using terminology grown from the soil of this passage. Every mom who withholds "the rod" in a moment of tenderness and compassion is silently challenging a prevailing Christian view that is derived from this passage. Every child who talks back to a parent at the grocery store and escapes immediate retribution seems to be living proof of the foolhardiness of sparing the rod. Even if there is no physical rod in your hand, there is a figurative rod in your head that colors your thinking about discipline. That's why it's impossible to ignore the "rod" passages in the book of Proverbs when we discuss God's design for childhood discipline.

Someone has said that confession is good for the soul, but bad for the reputation. So be it. I began raising my children as a "rod parent." But my discomfort with corporal punishment as the discipline of first resort, and my re-examination of the child rearing passages in Proverbs, changed my understanding of what the Bible teaches about childhood discipline. God does talk about physical discipline, but it's not what many of us assume it to be.

Sally and I started our marriage and family a bit later than usual, so I was thirty-three when our first child, Sarah, was born in 1984. I didn't enter parenthood uninformed, though. For ten years after graduating from college, I had been swimming in a sea of biblical input and Christian ministry. I served as a staff writer with Campus Crusade for Christ, participated for several years in a single-adults ministry in Texas, developed a music ministry as a songwriter and performer, and logged two years of graduate studies on my way to a master of divinity degree. During that time, I read many of the most popular Christian books on family and parenting, both classic and contemporary, absorbed the biblical perspectives of some of the best preachers and teachers in the country, and did much Bible study and thinking about the topic. Sally came to motherhood with much the same kind of exposure from her years in ministry. We thought we were well versed in the wisdom and ways of Christian parenting.

Here's what I thought I knew: The rod is God's ordained method of disciplining young children. Without physical discipline, which is what I took the rod to symbolize, a child would become a rebel and a tyrant. It was a formula: Spank your children to love them and to save their souls; avoid spanking only if you hate your children and want to encourage their spiritual death. Physical discipline was the one thing that would drive out the foolishness that is bound up in a child's heart. There was, to be sure, a wide range of other acceptable methods, but somehow they weren't supported with the same degree of biblical authority that the rod passages commanded. In my personal toolbox of discipline methods, I resorted to physical discipline as the "last resort" method, reserved for the correction of outright rebellion, defiance, and willful disobedience. However, when other methods failed, I knew with biblical assurance that physical punishment was God's method of choice.

My head knowledge about discipline didn't really get tested until Sarah was beyond toddlerhood and moving into childhood. At that point I felt it was time to get serious about doing discipline the right way, so I made a paddle. Although Scripture is silent on paddles, none of the books I had read seriously suggested using an actual rod. But the other alternatives didn't measure up: A switch was too silly (my grandmother used willow switches), a wooden spoon had no real authority, a belt conjured up images of angry, merciless whippings in the toolshed, and I'd heard too many times not to use your hand, which should be associated only with love. So I decided a paddle was the closest equivalent to the Bible's rod. When it came to actually making a paddle, though, I had no biblical guidance, so I used the only model I'd ever seen, which was the paddle my high school gym teacher used—the proverbial "Board of Education."

For the next ten years or so, as two boys and another baby girl arrived in our family, the paddle was a fixture in my toolbox of disciplinary methods. It was mostly a silent threat, though, often accomplishing its work without leaving its place in the closet. Since the question, "Do you need a spanking?" usually sufficed, I only infrequently resorted to the paddle, and even then its use was usually limited to a single swat, always administered on clothed bottoms, always in private, and never in anger. The terrible sting of the "lick" given years ago by my gym teacher—and the humiliation of having to bend over in front of a roomful of friends—was still fresh in my memory. I spanked my kids only rarely and always gently, yet the same question inevitably surfaced: Is this really what God had in mind?

As much as I preferred other methods, I used the paddle for one reason only: I believed it was God's ordained method of disciplining children. I didn't want to be disobedient to God in my role as a father, and I certainly didn't want to contribute to my children's becoming rebels. And yet my spirit was deeply troubled every time I used the paddle. It didn't seem to fit the character of God or be consistent with the nature of a loving parent. It didn't seem to be proportional discipline for a young child. Neither did it seem to have sufficient biblical support. In short, it just didn't seem right.

Unfortunately, I could think of only one Christian author at the time who held a "contrarian" view of physical discipline, but his teachings were not widely known, and they didn't go far enough in providing a defensible biblical position. I read dozens of Christian books and articles written since the 1970s. Many quoted the rod passages from Proverbs and suggested that physical discipline was, in some way, a divine mandate. Others simply acknowledged those passages and offered personal, extrabiblical advice on how best to spank children. Some claimed that a parent who wouldn't spank his children was being disobedient to God and actually hated his own children. A few books suggested spanking even infants! One suggested that the rod relieved a child's guilt from sin, serving as a kind of parentally imposed penitence or humiliation. Others proposed attractive alternative approaches but simply ignored the rod passages, as though those verses didn't exist. My reading made me wonder if I should ignore my inner concerns, resign myself to the common view, and keep my hand on the paddle.

ASKING NEW, AND NECESSARY, QUESTIONS

Somewhere in the mid-nineties, as my oldest child was entering young adulthood, my growing concerns led me to ask some new questions: "Who is the *child* referred to in Proverbs? What is the rod? Does God command the physical discipline of young children? Can I claim Proverbs verses about children as promises of God?" As I began to research the passages, talk to seminary professors, and scour the rest of the Scriptures for clues, my convictions grew stronger that there was another way to look at these passages. When we English speakers hear the word *child,* we think of a school-age youngster. In conservative Christian circles, *child* refers to a school-age youngster or even a toddler. But is that how a Jew in the time of Solomon would have understood the word in Hebrew? My studies suggested otherwise.

Train Up a Child at What Age?

Like a key that opens a locked door, Proverbs 22:6 is important for understanding not only the rod passages of Proverbs but also the bigger picture of biblical discipline: "Train up a child in the way he should go, even when he is old he will not depart from it." Respected teachers of God's Word disagree on just what this verse means, but three interpretive versions have held the hill longest.

The first and most common interpretation maintains that parents should begin the spiritual training of their children at a young age because the training will stay with them for a lifetime. This view is generally used to assure the parents of potential (and actual) prodigals that, if they start early enough, their children will eventually return to their parents' faith.

The second view teaches that you should spiritually train a young child "according to his way." In other words, raise him according to the personality and abilities God has given him, and when he is old he will remain true to that bent.

Finally, there is the interpretation that says "train up" is derived from an older term meaning to "touch the palate," referring to how a Hebrew mother would train a child to desire solid food. This view promotes the idea of creating appetites for God early in a child's life. If that is done, the thinking goes, those appetites will remain there for life.

Here is a fourth interpretation that I find to be a simpler, clearer way to understand this passage. Let's look at each of the key words. First, the specific Hebrew word translated as "train up" is used only four other times in the Old Testament, and in every situation it has to do not with training, but with the dedication of the temple or of a structure. Only in Proverbs 22:6 is the word *chanak* translated "train." Literally it means "to dedicate." Next, the word translated as "way" in this verse is a form of the word *derek,* which is used consistently in the Old Testament to mean the "way of wisdom," the "way of life," or the "way of righteousness" (see Proverbs 4:11, 6:23, 10:29) or its opposite, the "way of the wicked" or the "way of a fool" (see Proverbs 2:12, 4:19, 12:15). It is a term of moral direction and commitment. Proverbs 30:18-20 uses *derek* as a comparative—"The way of an eagle in the sky, the way of a serpent on a rock"—but this is a less common use of the word, which is used at least seventy-five times in Proverbs to refer to the way of life. Then, the word used for "old" in Proverbs 22:6 normally refers to an elder, but here the verb means simply to grow older.[2] It comes from a root word that means "beard," so it can also indicate simply reaching mature adulthood. Next, the word translated as "depart" means just that, but I prefer its more common and more descriptive meaning, "to turn away."

Finally, we come to the word in this verse that is translated "child," the Hebrew word *naar*. This term is used in the Old Testament to refer to a wide range of ages, from an infant to an adult. However, Scripture most commonly uses *naar* to mean "young man" or "youth," often determined by the immediate text or context, but usually indicating adolescent years up to marriageable age. Jewish rabbinical tradition considered a *naar* to be between the ages of sixteen and twenty-four.[3] This definition is supported by several Old Testament examples: Joseph was a *naar* at age seventeen when he was sold into slavery by his brothers (see Genesis 37:27-28); Joshua was a *naar* probably in his late teens at Sinai and when he spied out the Promised Land (see Exodus 33:11); David, the young shepherd able to slay a lion but not yet able to wear Saul's armor, was a *naar* when he killed Goliath (see 1 Samuel 17:42); Solomon was a *naar* in his late teens prior to taking the throne at around age twenty-one (see 1 Chronicles 22:5); Absalom was a *naar* when he killed his brother Amnon (see 2 Samuel 14:21); Josiah was a *naar* at age sixteen when he began to seek God (see 2 Chronicles 34:3); and the *naar* mentioned in Psalms 119:9 is surely a young adult wrestling with sexual purity ("How can a young man keep his way pure?").

A Fresh Look at Training Children

With this background in mind, let's take a fresh look at Proverbs 22:6, reading it with this layman's paraphrase: "Dedicate a young man to following God's way of wisdom. Even when he is a grown man, he will not turn aside from that way." As I put these words together the first time, the passage took on an entirely new meaning. No longer was it speaking about a small child, but about a young man. No longer did it address general childhood "character training." Instead the call was to set a young man's feet on the path of righteousness and wisdom during his adolescence or young adulthood. No longer did the verse imply the perspective of an entire lifetime, but of the training that is preparation for becoming an adult, a mature member of the faith community.

The passage actually describes a young man who has left childhood behind and who is ready to follow God on his own and prepare to enter the adult world—but his parents need to dedicate him to that path. In the same way we dedicate a church building to God's use when it has been completed, according to this passage, we should dedicate our youth to God's purposes once their childhood has been completed. This soon-to-be-adult member of the community of faith, who is now entering young adulthood, must be dedicated and put to use for his or her intended purpose. That is the *naar* described in this passage.

I did all twelve units of my seminary Hebrew studies in one very difficult summer, but it's not difficult to see that this passage is key to understanding the rod passages in Proverbs. If the *naar* of Proverbs 22:6 was not a young child but a young man, then the rod passages of Proverbs need a fresh look because the same words are in view.

A Closer Look at the Rod

For most of my parenting years, I believed that God had decreed the rod of physical discipline to be His only authorized method of discipline. Even though I didn't use physical discipline often, I used it misguidedly because of my incomplete understanding of Scripture. Physical discipline of young children is not prohibited. God nowhere says, "Thou shalt not spank." However, it's clear that neither is it commanded or even suggested in Scripture. We need to take a fresh look at what the Bible actually teaches about childhood discipline.

Before we examine the various "rod" passages, it's important to put the book of Proverbs in context. Proverbs is not a book that recounts history or tells a story. Rather, it is a collection of wise sayings compiled by Solomon, David's son, and other wise men of the time. Proverbs are poetic expressions of wisdom for living and for pleasing God.

One of the first sticky issues to confront, then, is the nature of the truth found in Proverbs. Are proverbial commands meant to be obeyed in the same way we obey commands given directly by God or Jesus? Are proverbial promises, such as the implied promise of Proverbs 22:6, meant to be claimed? I have found it best to read the Proverbs in the spirit that they are often quoted and used in the New Testament—as God-inspired practical wisdom for living righteously and skillfully. Rather than commands, they are counsel; rather than promises, they are principles; rather than moral imperatives, they are divine guidance. In that sense, they are in the same spirit as the parables of Jesus—containing, reflecting, and picturing divine truth and wisdom for the listener or reader, but not intended as divine imperatives or promises. In the same way that Jesus told parables to arrest His hearers' attention and make a point about God and His kingdom, the wisdom writers of the Old Testament used proverbs to make a point about living well according to God's ways.

Another important observation about the context of the book concerns the intended audience. In the first nine chapters, Solomon addressed his son or sons with admonitions to follow the way of righteousness in the same way that the boy's (or boys') parents have stayed on God's path. It's clear that this young man, "my son," is reaching the age at which he can be tempted by wayward friends, the bed of the harlot, and the pursuit of ill-gotten wealth. The son is a young man in that difficult transition between childhood and manhood. Though the wisdom of Proverbs is addressed to all people, there is a special emphasis on training the young, turning them from folly, and setting their feet on the path of wisdom and righteousness. Solomon stated that the purpose of the book, in part, is "to give prudence to the naive, to the youth *(naar)* knowledge and discretion" (Proverbs 1:4).

Finally, there is a kind of hidden context that will affect how we read the rod passages. Proverbs is all about choices—choosing between wisdom and foolishness, righteousness and wickedness, discipline and laziness. It is about being able to discern between the things of God (wisdom) and the things of the world (folly) and making the right choice. The hidden assumption underlying all of these choices is that the "chooser" is capable of wise discernment. This is not, as we considered in the previous chapter, a quality of young children, who have not yet reached the point at which they know enough "to refuse evil and choose good" (Isaiah 7:15). Proverbs addresses and describes those who have moved beyond childhood and into young adulthood or full adulthood, those who are morally capable and culpable for their lives and choices.

Rethinking the Rod

Looking at Proverbs in context helps us discern what the rod passages are really saying. Eight passages in Proverbs refer to the rod, of which only four are generally applied to the discipline of children. Let's start with the four that are rarely quoted:

- "On the lips of the discerning, wisdom in found, but a rod *[shebet]* is for the back of him who lacks understanding" (10:13).
- "In the mouth of the foolish is a rod *[choter]* for his back, but the lips of the wise will protect them" (14:3).
- "He who sows iniquity will reap vanity, and the rod *[shebet]* of his fury will perish" (22:8).
- "A whip is for the horse, a bridle for the donkey, and a rod *[shebet]* for the back of fools" (26:3).

Since the plain reading of these passages shows that they refer to an adult—and a foolish adult at that—we won't delve into a detailed analysis of these verses.[4] Instead, we'll look at the verses more commonly understood to apply to children. The following passages from Proverbs are the ones most often quoted to promote the notion that physical discipline of young children is a divine mandate:

- "He who withholds his rod *[shebet]* hates his son *[ben]*, but he who loves him disciplines him diligently" (13:24).
- "Foolishness is bound up in the heart of a child *[naar]*; the rod *[shebet]* of discipline will remove it far from him" (22:15).

- "Do not hold back discipline from the child *[naar]*, although you strike him with the rod *[shebet]*, he will not die. You shall strike him with the rod *[shebet]* and rescue his soul from Sheol" (23:13-14).

- "The rod *[shebet]* and reproof give wisdom, but a child *[naar]* who gets his own way brings shame to his mother" (29:15).

Rather than give a commentary on each passage, it's better to make some observations about the four verses as a group. Consider these crucial points:

First, the "child" in each passage is not a young child, but a young man. We have been culturally conditioned to read these verses as applying to a young child, but it's time to read these passages through a lens of new understanding. The recipient of the discipline is best understood as a young man *(naar)*, probably in his mid- to late teens, walking on the path that takes him from childhood into adulthood. Although Proverbs 13:24 uses the word *ben,* a common Hebrew word for "son" or "child" with no reference to age, there is nothing to suggest that it, too, should be anything other than a young man.[5]

Second, the rod *(shebet)* in these passages is real, not symbolic. In most cases, about 180 in the Old Testament, *shebet* is translated "tribe" or "scepter." The rod or scepter held by a king or ruler represented both his authority and those under his authority. In some thirty verses, though, *shebet* clearly means a rod or a club, an instrument of punishment, correction, and judgment that brings pain and physical wounds to the receiver (see Psalm 89:32). In Numbers 24:17 the *shebet* of the coming Messiah will "crush through the forehead of Moab," picturing much more than a little wand or a gilded stick. In Exodus 21:20, the *shebet* can kill a man. In Psalm 23, the *shebet* in the hands of the shepherd is an effective weapon to protect the sheep from lions and bears (see verse 4). At the time of the writing of Proverbs, the *shebet* was commonly understood to be an instrument used to inflict pain. Nothing in these passages, or in the context of Proverbs, suggests that these references to the rod should be spiritualized to mean only "authority" or taken as a symbol of other forms of physical discipline.

Third, nowhere else in Scripture is the rod as an instrument of punishment or discipline ever associated with a young child. Scripture refers to the "little ones" and young children as innocent and under the protection of adults, in part because they don't yet know right from wrong (in the sense of being culpable for that knowledge). Throughout Scripture the rod is an instrument of judgment and punishment for those who have made moral choices in rebellion against God or His ways. It is always, without exception, associated with youth, adults, and nations.

Fourth, although it may be true that a young child's heart seems full of foolishness, that is not the point of Proverbs 22:15, which has a "young man" in view. Foolishness in Proverbs is not the same as the natural immaturity of a young child, a condition that is not condemned by Scripture. Rather, "foolishness" refers to the folly and stupidity of an otherwise mature youth or adult who willfully rejects God's wisdom and ways. The overriding theme and admonition of Proverbs is "The fear of the LORD is the beginning of knowledge; fools despise wisdom and instruction" (Proverbs 1:7). In layman's terms, "Follow God and be wise; reject God and be the fool." That admonition in Proverbs is directed only to those who are morally responsible before God and especially to youth (1:4) who are in immediate need of "knowledge and discretion" as they move toward adulthood. In contrast, young children are not considered fools when they do wrong; they are simply immature and childish because they are children.

Fifth, these passages make much better sense when "child" is understood as "youth" or "young man." In the culture around the time of Solomon, the notion of wielding a rod across the back of a rebellious slave to force him to submit would have been familiar (see Exodus 21:20-21). Was Solomon saying that Hebrew fathers should consider using the rod on their rebellious sons? Yes, I'd say that's exactly what he was saying. The Law provided that a "stubborn and rebellious" son could be stoned to death

(Deuteronomy 21:18-21). Perhaps that same idea is behind the words of Proverbs 23:13-14, that the young man disciplined with the rod "will not die" and his soul will be rescued from Sheol. Should we then use the rod on rebellious sons today? No, I think not. The cultural context of those words is separated from our day by three thousand years. We are no longer bound to the Old Testament Law (for instance, we don't stone rebellious sons). We are instead guided by the liberty and grace of the New Covenant, made possible by the shed blood of Jesus on our behalf. Nonetheless, it's still true that a rebellious and undisciplined son brings "shame to his mother" (Proverbs 29:15). So should we be just as serious in dealing with rebellious sons today as Solomon suggests? Yes, emphatically so! But we need to discipline our sons in light of the rest of Scripture, which was not available to Solomon. There is so much more to biblical discipline, as we will see in the chapters that follow, than what is found in a few passages in Proverbs.

Finally, it's not a stretch to say that the greatest spiritual need in a young man's life, after coming into a saving relationship with Jesus Christ, is discipline. However, if you hear the word *discipline* and think only "punishment," you're missing most of the biblical picture. Punishment may be a necessary part of discipline, but there is much more to discipline than an occasional knock upside the head (or across the back). The biblical picture of discipline in Proverbs is the entire process that sets young men's, or young women's, feet on the path of righteousness and helps keep them there until they are walking that path as mature adults. To understand the Bible's teaching on discipline, especially as it relates to young children, we must consider its bigger meaning, which includes direction, correction, and protection. As I've said, I call this approach "heartfelt discipline."

WHERE THE BIBLICAL TEACHING LEADS US

Let's return to the initial questions that sent me on my search for biblical truth about discipline: Who is the child in Proverbs? What is the rod? Does

God command the physical discipline of young children? Can I claim the outcomes mentioned in Proverbs as promises from God? And where does all of this leave us? To follow is what I have concluded.

Who Is the Child in Proverbs?

The "child" is really a young man or a youth, not a youngster. The book of Proverbs was written for adults, whether they be young adults taking the first steps out of childhood and into adulthood or mature adults who need wisdom for living life skillfully and well.

What Is the Rod?

The rod is an instrument of punishment and correction. It's not a switch or a paddle or a dowel or a wooden spoon. If you accept the rod passages of Proverbs as a divine mandate for disciplining young children and you take those passages literally, you'll find yourself beating your child with a heavy stick or branch.

Does God Command the Physical Discipline of Young Children?

Simply put, children are not in view in these passages. We'll see in the chapters that follow that neither the Old Testament nor the New Testament addresses the physical discipline of young children.[6]

Can I Claim Outcomes Mentioned in Proverbs As Promises of God?

Wisdom literature should not be read as a collection of divine promises for us to claim. The wise man of Proverbs is not instructed to claim them, but rather he is described as one who listens to them, learns from them, applies them, and increases in discernment and wisdom (see Proverbs 1:1-7). You would not be wise to claim a proverb as an unassailable promise of God. You would only be wise to apply it to your life as good counsel.

Where Does All of This Leave Us?

I'm still filling in the missing parts, but I see the Bible and my children in ways I had completely missed before. When I finally began to "spare the rod," I naturally wondered about the biblical alternative to rod-based discipline. Answering that question has shown me not only a heart-oriented approach to discipline, but also a biblical *relationship* with my children. I was missing the relational part of discipline that would enable me to open and to win my children's hearts; I was missing the biblical picture of discipline as a journey along a path with my children; and I was missing the life of the Holy Spirit in the discipline and training of my children.

Once I set out on the course of heartfelt discipline, I then had to ask: *Will the absence of physical discipline be the cause of rebellion? Can a child become mature and wise if a parent avoids physical discipline?* I began to think harder and study longer to see what God's Word really has to say. I was seeking a form of discipline that would shape my children's hearts to live for God. I found the answer in Scripture, but it wasn't at all what I was expecting.

CHAPTER 4

PARENTING BY FAITH

The Bible's Formula-Free Approach to Discipline

If spanking is not stamped with the official Biblical Child Raising seal of approval, then what method is? If the Bible doesn't teach that physical discipline is the divinely mandated approach, then what rules should we follow?

When my younger son was going through his preadolescent years, he would occasionally experience an emotional meltdown that expressed itself in anger and an argumentative spirit. Since he was an extrovert as well as a verbally and physically expressive child, these episodes tested my resolve. An inner voice would repeat axioms I'd heard about parents being in control, being consistent in discipline, and needing to establish parental authority. If my son is testing my parental authority (and he was), then it's my duty to make sure he knows just who is the boss. It was a battle of wills, and I needed to make sure my will won the battle. How could I interpret my son's emotional meltdown in any way other than he was asking to be punished?

During one of his outbursts, I reached for the paddle and heard myself saying things like, "If you can't control yourself, then you're asking me to control you... I'll have to give an accounting to God if I don't spank you... This isn't punishment; it's discipline... Now, bend over and take your discipline like a man." We both cried, and as I comforted him after the spanking, there was a stinging sense in my spirit that causing my young child that kind of pain was not natural. As I thought back on each incident, I realized that my justifications for spanking consisted of clichés and maxims, not God's words or the wisdom of Scripture. I felt as though I was acting according to someone else's rules. Sure, most spankings got results, but my son's response came from a defeated heart, not a humbled one. It was little more than an "I win, you lose" settlement.

On a different occasion, although the circumstances and my son's attitude were the same, I chose a different path. Instead of reaching for the paddle, I decided to reach inside, and I asked God to help me reach the heart of my child. I knew this wouldn't be the quick fix of harsher punishment that uses parental power to silence all dissent and discussion. I was reaching for a fuller expression of discipline, a biblical path to my son's heart.

Part of me just wanted to yell at my son in a fed-up-father voice and force a conclusion to the situation. But instead I decided to respond gently and lovingly to my child's anger and sullenness. We went to his room where I had him lie on his bed and cool off. I let him express his anger and frustration. An immature attitude had precipitated his meltdown, and emotion had been speaking, not reason. I let him know that I understood what he was going through, having once been a preadolescent myself. Then I began to give him some biblical perspectives on the situation, responding to his frustrations with reason, confronting the sin of his actions and attitudes with Scripture. I lovingly corrected him and counseled him on what he needed to do—confess his sin to God and ask forgiveness of those he had offended. Nothing was forced by threat of punishment or pain; repentance was drawn out by relationship. Over the course of an hour, his spirit changed, and there emerged a genuine conviction of sin and a real desire to do better. As we left the room, I felt closer to my son, and I could see his humbled heart. It was a win-win outcome.

WHO IS IN CONTROL?

The point of telling that story is not to suggest that there is only one way to discipline your children. There may come a time when talk needs to turn to action in order for parents to reach a child's heart. But before making that decision, we need to think about who is in control of the situation. I don't mean either you or your child. An immature child should never be in control of a mature adult. God has delegated to parents authority over their children (see Deuteronomy 5:16). Children are to show respect to their parents in the same way they are to show respect and honor to God. Paul emphasizes that children are to obey their parents "in all things" and that doing so pleases God (Colossians 3:20). Although God has given you authority over your children, that doesn't mean that their first response to you will always be complete, joyous obedience, any more than such joy typifies your response to God's discipline in your own life. Respect does mean, though, that the ultimate result of your loving, patient, and gentle discipline will be a child with a humble and obedient heart who honors your authority. As you exercise biblical discipline, you show your child what God the Father is like.

There is a separate issue of control in parenting, though, and that concerns who or what is in control of *you*. When you discipline your children, three primary sources of control can come into play: flesh, formula, and faith. You can allow one or all of these to guide how you relate to your children, but most parents gravitate toward one over the others.

Discipline by the Flesh

Scripture warns us against the sins of the flesh, the lusts of the flesh, and the acts of the flesh. Sadly, the flesh often controls a parent's words, actions, and attitudes toward his or her children. Nothing good comes from the flesh, which is the sinful part of our natures, the part that is lawless and resistant to God. Parents who don't know Christ have no real option other than to parent by flesh. They may be able to counterfeit godly, biblical discipline, but the source is still the unredeemed, sinful self. Though their discipline may even be loving and effective, if it doesn't derive from and lead to God, it is fleshly and vain. It is discipline that leads not to life in Christ, but to death in the flesh.

Christian parents have the Spirit of God dwelling within them. The hard truth, though, is that God doesn't remove our sinful natures when we find salvation in Christ. I may no longer be enslaved to my flesh, but it's still there. I know I should consider myself "dead to sin, but alive to God in Christ Jesus," and my daily desire should be to give myself to God as an "instrument of righteousness," freed from slavery to sin to serve Christ. However, I can—and do—choose to "let sin reign" in my life, and I sometimes allow my body to be used as an "instrument of unrighteousness" (see Romans 6:8-14). That happens when I give in to the urge to yell at my children when what they really need is biblical discipline. I give in to the flesh when I use my authority to lord it over my children just like rulers who don't know God (see Jesus' description of them in Matthew 20:25-28). It's the fleshly part of me that says, "I can make my kids submit to me by using the force of my will and the strength of my own hand." Even though my children may conform to my wishes, I have put confidence in my sinful self rather than in the leading of God's Spirit. When I do that, my discipline is no more effective or spiritual than that of a non-Christian parent.

Discipline by Formula

The second common method of discipline puts its faith in a false belief— that there exists a foolproof parenting formula—rather than relying on the sovereignty of God and the leading of His Spirit. We see this in parents who are unswervingly committed to a simple, one-size-fits-all approach. A primary example: "Got a problem? Get the paddle!" How much simpler could it get? This narrow view creates spiritual blinders, preventing parents from seeing what Scripture says about the parent-child relationship and about issues of discipline beyond immediate correction.

In our years of parenting and of ministering to families, Sally and I have found that most parents want simple instructions, an easy secret to successful parenting that will solve even their most vexing discipline quandaries. I could say they're looking for "Ten Steps to Biblical Parenting," but in our time-challenged culture even five steps is probably pushing it. When there is so little time left in many parents' busy days for children, the drive for the disciplinary "quick fix" is strong. After the parents' heart cry of "just tell me what to do," there usually follows a whispered, "and how to do it *fast!*"

These how-to steps are exactly what many parenting experts, Christian and secular alike, attempt to provide. Each offers an apparently authoritative approach to discipline—a formula. Whether they latch on to one or two scriptures that become the sine qua non of Christian parenting, or they extrapolate an approach from between the lines of Scripture, or they develop a biblically centered personal opinion about discipline, the result is a formula. Parents who quickly reach for a paddle have found a formula that is much easier to follow than figuring out and following their own redeemed, Spirit-directed instincts. Spanking, after all, is quick and easy, perfect for the busy American lifestyle.

In our efforts to find a universal formula for effective and efficient discipline, we parents can convince ourselves that, if an expert's approach is right for us, then it must be right for everybody. At that point we begin to create a body of "Christian law." Just like the Pharisees, who started out with good intentions about wanting to keep God's Law, we soon find ourselves trying to live up to a standard that God did not define and, worse, insisting that others live up to it too, judging their parenting standards by our own. That—trying to do right by keeping all the rules—of course, is legalism. Keeping my own or someone else's law is not the path to biblical parenting. When we discipline by formula, we put our confidence in a set of rules rather than trusting in God, who knows our hearts and the hearts of our children.

Discipline by Faith

There is no universal formula for Christian parenting. It's a family-by-family, day-by-day walk of faith. And perhaps nowhere are we challenged to walk by faith more than in disciplining our children. But when we discover the biblical pattern of discipline by faith, we are freed from the tyranny of flesh and formula. We've lived so long with the notion that there *must* be a simple biblical formula, we can't imagine raising young children without an easy-to-follow list of rules. But if you understand the nature of the Christian life, you'll begin to see that discipline by faith is as much an issue of your own maturity and trust in God as it is an issue of how to discipline your children. Discipline by faith has to do with walking in the Spirit (see Galatians 5:16; Ephesians 5:15-18; Colossians 2:6-7), and that's the essence of the Christian life.

Sally and I both were involved with Campus Crusade for Christ first as college students and then as full-time staff after graduation. Though its ministry is multifaceted, Campus Crusade is still probably known best for its evangelistic tract "The Four Spiritual Laws." Every staff member is trained in how to share his or her faith using that tool. However, while we were constantly reminded of our responsibility to have a personal witness, we were also taught that the effectiveness of our witness depended on the power of the Holy Spirit in our lives. I learned early on proven techniques for turning a conversation to Christ, how to use the best illustrations and anecdotes, and how to be a great "closer" when asking for a decision. But, most important, I learned that I could fail miserably in my witness if I did it in my own power. The only things in life that matter are those done in the power of the Holy Spirit (see 2 Corinthians 3:1-6).

Even after Sally and I left staff and started a family, we couldn't escape the idea of walking in the power of the Holy Spirit—except when we walked in the front door of our home to be parents. When it came to the question of how to discipline our young children, we lived as though we believed that the Holy Spirit was not involved in our parenting. It was as though we preferred the advice of a human "expert" to the inner prompting of God's Spirit. We stopped relying on God for wisdom and started relying on others or on ourselves. It took several years for us to understand the power of formula-free, Spirit-led, faith-based discipline. And it changed how we parent.

After years of relying on everything but the Spirit of God, we finally realized that God wanted us to live by faith when it came to raising our children. He wanted us to depend on Him—on the power of His Spirit and the wisdom of His Word—rather than on formulas, experts, or our parenting skills. It's not flesh or formula that will make us effective, but faith—living in the power of the Holy Spirit who is working moment by moment in our hearts to help us be more like Christ. Isn't that what we want our children to see—Christ in us, especially in our discipline? That is a biblical truth so simple and radical that it can change how you look at all of life, but especially at your life at home with your children.

THE HOLY SPIRIT'S CONTROL OF YOUR LIFE

If the idea of disciplining by faith makes you uncomfortable, maybe you haven't considered how the ministry of the Holy Spirit affects the ministry of parenting. What follows is an abbreviated summary of what the Bible says about living in the Spirit, especially as it concerns your life as a parent and the issues of childhood discipline. The Bible shows us that discipline is a dynamic relationship between parent, child, and God. Understanding that relationship will change how you think about discipline.

Your Life Is No Longer Your Own
When you trust Christ for your salvation, everything changes because the God of the universe has taken over your heart. What you once were is

gone; what you are now is in the hands of the God of creation who has come to re-create you into something entirely new. God is intimately and constantly involved in everything you do as a parent. If the Holy Spirit is active in your heart, then you can't approach any part of parenting casually or carelessly. What God is doing in you will change your children's lives, but what you do as a parent whose heart belongs to God will also change your life. God, through the Holy Spirit, is not only working through you, but in you as you live for Him at home.

You Become a New Person

The Holy Spirit is not passive. Making you a "new creation" is just the beginning of His work because He then sets about the task of conforming your new nature to the likeness of Christ. The Holy Spirit is at work in your new nature, changing you to be more like Christ. You will continue to grow in your understanding of how God wants you to relate to your children. Because children are people, parenting is a dynamic and always-changing process in the same way that spiritual growth is a dynamic process. As you become more like Christ, your children should be the first to be touched by that change.

You Must Choose to Live Like a New Creation

The one catch in the Christian life is that you still have to live with your sinful nature. It doesn't go away when the Holy Spirit makes you a new creation. Your new nature is not a guarantee of sinless perfection, but it is a divine provision that enables you to say no to sinful impulses and desires and instead say yes to God. It's a deliberate choice. When your child does something that really ticks you off, frustrates you because you don't know what to do, or seems to be challenging your authority, it's hard to know whether your response is from the flesh or from the Spirit. But that's when you need to remember that parenting is a spiritual matter, and you need to choose to listen to and follow the Spirit in your heart.

We Can Discipline by Faith Only with the Help of God's Spirit

There is only one way that any of us can live the Christian life, and that is by the power of the Holy Spirit. Everything about your old nature is fleshly and sinful; only your new nature in the Holy Spirit can live the Christian life. Why? Because that is the only part of you that is able to become like Christ while you live in an earthly body. Anything you do that is not done in the Spirit is done in the flesh and is worthless.[1] The only way to keep from living in the flesh is to live, or "walk," in the Spirit. To many Christians, that sounds mystical. How do you know when you're walking in the Spirit? It's not that hard, really. First, be sure you've confessed any known sins. Your heart has to be right with God. Second, saturate your life with the Word of God. The Holy Spirit speaks to your heart mostly with the words of Scripture. Third, talk to God by letting prayer become a part of your thought processes all day long. Finally, don't live in fear of displeasing God, but live in faith that pleases Him. Believe that He is living in you, guiding you, and helping you—and then live as though you really believe it. That's living by faith. For parents, living by the power of the Spirit is not a goal; it is an absolute necessity.

The Holy Spirit Sets You Free from the Flesh and Formula

Christians, especially in America, struggle with two things: flesh and formula. We are constantly drawn by the urges of our sinful nature, and we're constantly seeking ways to make life easier and more efficient. Most Christians know when they're choosing to sin by giving in to the flesh. However, it's much less apparent when we choose to live by the law of a surefire formula.

The Law must have seemed like a formula for the Jews, freshly freed from slavery in Egypt. At Sinai God gave them a codified law that would make them a physical nation with a spiritual purpose. Though He never intended it to be a formula for righteous living, over time that's how the people came to view it. Though the Law had its place, God's standard of acceptance has always been faith, not works.[2]

Christ came to perfectly fulfill the righteous and moral requirements of the Law and to provide the means by which God's law would be written on the hearts of His people by His Spirit. The means of this salvation would be faith, not works—believing in Christ and accepting His sacrifice, not doing good things to earn God's acceptance. Salvation would be an unmerited gift of God's grace, not favor earned. But the grip of law-based righteousness is not easily broken. Even though Paul clearly taught that God meant for the Law to be only a tutor to reveal our sin and to point us to Christ, the early church still could not resist the urge to create new standards of righteousness. Living by faith, walking in the Spirit, following the law of love—these were internal standards of righteousness that only God, who can see into the heart, can measure. Many in the new church wanted additional standards that were tangible and visible, external standards that they themselves could measure and judge. Instead, Paul exhorted, the only way to live the life of Christ, and to not "carry out the desire of the flesh," was to be controlled by the Spirit of God, to "walk by the Spirit" and lead a life characterized by the "fruit of the Spirit" (see Galatians 5:16,22-23).

Paul's admonition to the early church is still relevant today: "It was for freedom that Christ set us free; therefore keep standing firm [that is, in faith] and do not be subject again to a yoke of slavery" (Galatians 5:1). The urge not only to wear the yoke of slavery consisting of man-made formulas, but also to place it on others, is still strong. And the answer is still the same: "Walk by the Spirit, and you will not carry out the desire of the flesh" (Galatians 5:16). There is no law that can control by external standards of behavior what is in the internal reaches of the heart. Only the Spirit of God can do that.

As a Christian, you are free to follow the Spirit in your parenting. There are many who will try to create a Christian law of childhood discipline, and they will try to burden you with its yoke, but you don't have to wear it. The reality of the Holy Spirit working in your life is the promise of formula-free discipline. There is no law you have to follow—only the leading of the Holy Spirit and the Word of God. God is working in you, and He is committed to helping you with your children. You simply need to let Him. So stand firm in your faith and don't be subject to a yoke of formula.

Godly Parents Live by the Power of the Spirit

Parenting is a much bigger part of the Christian life than most of us care to admit. Under your care are eternal beings whose courses for eternity will be set, in large measure, by what you do. Who and what they become will be shaped by how you relate to them, discipline them, instruct them, counsel them, and love them. What they believe and think about God will be influenced by the God they see in you.

When I think about this, I'm struck by how utterly dependent I need to be on God. I want as much of Him in my parenting as possible. I need God's help to be a "supernatural" parent! That means learning to live by faith in the power of the Spirit and resisting the bondage of both flesh and formula. Here's the bottom line: I can't be a truly Christian parent without the life of Christ in my parenting. That comes only by the Holy Spirit.

THE HOLY SPIRIT'S CONTROL OF YOUR CHILD'S LIFE

If parenting by faith is dependent on the power of the Spirit, then what is the Spirit's role in our children's lives? Is the important thing that they come to know Christ and then exhibit the traits of Christian character?

In the early years of our parenting, Sally and I were drawn to the idea of Christian character training. Plenty of parenting resources showed how to build different character qualities into a growing child's life. But many of these approaches, if not most, relied on faulty assumptions. Without intending to, many of the resources encouraged parents to think like humanistic behaviorist psychologist B. F. Skinner, who held that he could produce whatever type of child he wanted if he were given total control over the stimuli the child was exposed to. When parents slip into thinking that their primary responsibility is to form their children's character, they run the risk of becoming functional behaviorists.

Of course we'd never advocate Skinner's views, but without realizing it, we might slip into affirming his methodology. Consider three of the most common faulty assumptions:

- Good character is created by good character qualities.
- Good character is created by good parenting methods.
- Good character is created by good parents.

While there is some truth in each assumption, they all should be marked false. Let's see how these assumptions relate to the biblical picture of character.

Is Good Character Created by Good Character Qualities?

This idea emerges when we talk about training a child: "We're really working with Billy on self-control this week" or "I really need to help Mary learn to be more responsible." We tend to see character in terms of its parts rather than as a whole. That's why many parents seek out training materials that focus on specific character traits they want their children to develop. The assumption is that if they work on the various qualities individually, the cumulative result will be the instilling of character into their children.

Good character is every parent's desire, but Christian character is not simply the accumulation of good traits. The Bible speaks a lot about various qualities of godliness, but always in the context of those who know Christ. Certainly a child, in the innocence of childhood, can do things that have the appearance of good character. The image of God stamped on a child's soul gives her some sense of goodness. But until a child receives a new nature when she receives Christ as her Savior, nothing a parent does can create Christian character in her heart. You can, and should, cultivate the soil of your child's heart by teaching her how to do good, how to honor you, and how to want to please God, but none of that is truly Christian character. Apart from the work of the Holy Spirit in a child's life, the accumulation of character qualities will not add up to Christian character, which brings us to the second myth.

Is Good Character Created by Good Parenting Methods?

Efficiency and productivity are part of the American experience. We demand results. As new parents, Sally and I read widely and took in videos and workshops about developing character in children. We wanted to raise godly kids, and we wanted to do it fast! That was an era of Christianity that rejected the permissive methods of the 1950s and 1960s, methods that had spawned a generation of rebels. It was time we took back control of our children. Discipline was the battle strategy, and victory would be measured in character qualities. Dozens of newly minted character training products and programs reinforced the idea that if my children weren't developing character, I just needed to try a new method.

Whether it's a character development program or a video series on the best methods to use to build character, we're prone to rely on methods or techniques to do what only God can do. In many cases, the unspoken assumption is that the program or methods are finally going to do what God has failed to accomplish. The issue we need to confront is not whether we use methods (we all do), but whether we're trusting in the method or in God. There is a part of me that wants a program or method that will let me off the hook: Follow the instructions, put in the video, say the prayer, and then sit back and watch your child's character take shape. If I could put my trust in the method, though, why would I need to trust God? There is very little in Scripture that resembles a methodology for childhood character development and training, probably so that we'll keep our eyes on God rather than on a method. Neither accumulated character traits nor a foolproof method instills true Christian character, which brings us to the third myth.

Is Good Character Created by Good Parents?

When the latest "new" method for character training fails to do the job, or when the busyness of life prevents our being consistent with any method, most of us find ourselves uttering (or muttering) familiar words: "After all, character is more caught than taught." It's a catchall guilt reliever that covers inconsistency, lost opportunities, fumbled words, procrastination, and everything else that conspires to make a parent feel ineffective.

At the very heart of Christian maturity are the ideas that we are called to be "like Christ" (see Philippians 4:7-11) and that less mature believers learn from the godly model of the more mature (see Hebrews 13:7). When applied to parenting, this principle usually suggests that a parent's example rubs off on the child, and the character of the child reflects the parent's. Therefore, good character is "caught" from a good parent. The truth is, though, the "more caught than taught" maxim doesn't have much direct biblical support. Both in the Old and New Testaments, when the parental role in a child's life is explained, it is a call to actively instruct and train. There is nothing passive about it. It is more accurate biblically to say, "Good character is best caught when it is actively taught."

Of course there will be many aspects of character that your child will catch just from your example. There are good habits, principles, and values that your child will pick up from you. Unfortunately, she will also pick up the bad. The real question is whether the good aspects that they "catch" can rightly be called Christian character. Can the power of a good parental example alone create actual Christian character in your child?

The reality is very simple: *You* can't create Christian character in your children. Christian character comes only from Christ, and only a heart that is changed by the Holy Spirit can exhibit the character of Christ. Christian character is the fruit of the Holy Spirit in the life of a Christian—love, joy, peace, patience, kindness, goodness, faithfulness, gentleness, and self-control (see Galatians 5:22-23). It is the actual character of Christ that is expressed through a changed heart.

Most children come to the point of discernment about the spiritual condition of their hearts about the time they turn the corner from childhood into young adulthood. If at that point the child turns to God and accepts Christ, then his spirit is made new in Christ, and he begins the process of growing into the likeness of Christ by the power of the Spirit. It is only then that he begins to develop true Christian character because now Christ is working in his heart.

A MORE COMPLETE PICTURE OF DISCIPLINE

Theologians and academics like to speak of paradigms, those mental models we use to look at and make sense of the world we live in. When the model changes and we begin to see once-familiar things in a whole new way, that is called a paradigm shift. We are long overdue for a biblical paradigm shift in the way we look at Christian parenting and especially in the ways we discipline our children. It is my prayer that the biblical idea of the path of life will become a new paradigm for faith-based parenting that moves beyond simplistic formulas. We need to recover the idea of Spirit-led discipline of our children.

Paul admonished the Colossian church, "Therefore as you have received Christ Jesus the Lord, *so walk in Him,* having been firmly rooted and now being built up in Him and established in your faith, just as you were instructed, and overflowing with gratitude" (Colossians 2:6-7). Even though they knew Christ and were established in their faith, the believers at Colossae needed to be encouraged to keep walking in Christ. Standing still wasn't an option. As a Christian parent reading a book on Christian parenting and discipline, you probably also have a settled faith in Christ. But it's not enough to stand still on the path of life and tell your children how to get to where you want them to go or hope that other teachers will help them find the way. It's your responsibility. You must be walking that path and bringing your children with you.

Remember Jesus' parable of the sower and the seed?[3] If, as it had for the Colossians, the seed of truth has already found good root in the soil of your heart ("firmly rooted…established in your faith"), the life of Christ is growing in you ("built up in Him…as you were instructed"), and the fruit of Christ's Spirit is evident ("overflowing with gratitude"), then you are ready to begin with your children the exciting adventure of heartfelt discipline. What is true of you is what you want to be true of your children, and by God's design you are the one who will show them what it means to walk in Christ and live by faith. As you walk the path of life with your children, your life built up by Christ will be their model and you will be their guide. Heartfelt discipline is a lens, a way to see more clearly what God wants to do in your children's lives through you. But you must decide to start walking.

The chapters that follow will help you understand what heartfelt discipline looks like. This is not a handbook of things to do, but a heartbook of ways to think biblically about your role as a parent. Through the ministry of the Holy Spirit in your own life, you'll find many more ways to exercise heartfelt discipline in your own family than I can suggest in a few pages. The remaining chapters will address the core issues of childhood discipline around three biblical priorities: direction, correction, and protection. These priorities are grounded in Scripture, and they express most of what a Christian parent does in the process of childhood discipline. These three priorities comprise the heart of heartfelt discipline.

Directive Discipline is the process of lovingly leading your child along the path of life. The goal is to have your children follow you as you walk that path and to open and win their hearts along the way. The four faces that you present to your children—sympathy, encouragement, nurture, and instruction—are relational skills that enable you to relate to your children at a heart-to-heart level. They are skills for discipline that will open the door of a child's heart both to the direction you have to offer and to the correction that you must exercise.

The second priority is *Corrective Discipline,* the process of skillfully correcting your children when they sin. The four tools involved in this process are useful disciplinary methods that offer loving correction. These tools are spiritual, verbal, behavioral, and physical discipline. The goal of corrective discipline is to get your children back on the path of life after they sin. You correct their trajectory and return them to the path of righteousness. The goal is not just to stop them from wrongdoing, but to redirect them toward God.

The third priority, *Protective Discipline,* is the process of wisely watching over your children to protect them from harmful influences. You can build three "fences" in this process, fences around appetites, relationships, and various media. The goal of protective discipline is to discern the positive and the negative influences entering your children's lives and to guard what is going into their hearts. As the parent, you are the ultimate protective fence that will keep out destructive influences until your children reach young adulthood, the age at which they can begin to exercise a certain amount of discernment and self-control on their own.

So let's keep on walking. Turn the page and take a closer look at the role of directive discipline in the lives of our children.

✦

PART II

DIRECTIVE

DISCIPLINE

CHAPTER 5

Sympathy Versus Strictness

The Power of Listening and Understanding

Something about a whining child really sets my teeth on edge. And there was a time in my son Joel's childhood when he fell into a pattern of whining and complaining with irritating regularity. Whenever it started, my natural response was simply to say, "Stop whining! Either change your attitude right now or go to your room until you can." Regardless of what was causing Joel's unhappiness, I felt I needed to correct his response to it.

My approach changed after a family with several very young children visited us. The kids invaded Joel's room and dismantled several prized Lego creations that he kept on a shelf. After they left, Joel shifted into his whiny mode. Rather than issuing a brusque correction, though, Sally and I sat on the couch with him and sympathized with his sadness.

"You must be pretty upset about your Lego models," we told Joel. "That would make us mad, too. Can we help you put them back together?"

The whining stopped, and an hour or so later Joel showed us his repaired creations. We even noticed that our expression of sympathy affected his attitude for the next several days. It was a telling example as I was learning the power of basic sympathy in a child's life.

This isn't just an issue for young children, though. Sally remembers a time when our daughter Sarah was going through some preadolescent mood swings, becoming sour and argumentative without warning. Sally had put up with it long enough; she was ready to confront and correct our daughter's bad attitudes. But instead she brewed Sarah a cup of tea, put on some soothing music, and invited her to sit down and talk. It was the touch of sympathy Sarah needed. She poured out her heart, sharing frustrations and fears she had been keeping inside. Then she said, "Thank you for not being mad at me, Mom. I know I shouldn't have such bad attitudes. I'm sorry about all that."

THE FACE OF SYMPATHY

If heartfelt discipline is about putting a new, biblical face on childhood discipline (chapters 5–8), then let me recommend sympathy as the place to begin. You might be thinking, *My child needs a firm hand and good values a lot more than my sympathy!* As we discussed in a previous chapter, biblical discipline is about much more than simply controlling a child's behavior. It's about shaping the heart, which is why heartfelt discipline has sympathy at its root. I want my children to know beyond a doubt that, even when I'm exercising my authority as a parent, they'll find no better and no more loyal friend and confidant than me. Even when they do their worst and I must correct their wrongdoing, they still need to know that I'm completely on their side.

I want my children to expect from me the same thing I expect from my heavenly Father: Even when I feel His correcting hand, I know He will listen to me, understand me, and respond in love. I know He is aware of my weaknesses and wants to help me become more mature. In the same way, my children want to know that I understand the mix of emotions and thoughts that is swirling around in their immature minds. When my children look at my face, I want them to see not a scowling judge demanding perfect obedience, but rather a sympathetic parent who is committed to helping them grow to maturity. No matter how strong or displeasing the discipline may be, my expressions of sympathy will keep their hearts open to me. This is essential because without an openness of heart there is no real relationship.

It is sympathy, which is an expression of God's grace and love, that describes the heart attitude that is missing in much of our parenting. Both Jesus and Paul contrasted grace and law, teaching that God is concerned with the internal realm of our heart attitudes and desires, not just with our outward acts.[1] Similarly, we need to understand the contrast between sympathy and strictness, the desire to reach the heart versus the single-minded desire to control our children's behavior. If we understand sympathy, we'll be a step closer to understanding the idea of grace in our discipline.

As a younger parent, I probably would have considered *sympathy* to be a stealth word for permissive discipline. It conjured up pictures of little old ladies smiling sweetly at a cherubic but devilish little boy behaving at his worst. It also sounded a lot like pity. But that was before I started reading books by noted Christians from the late 1800s, a time of robust Christianity in America. Here's an example from *Hints on Child Training*, an 1890 book by H. Clay Trumbull, father of eight, leader in the American Sunday-school movement, and a prolific author and personal evangelist:

> It is unquestionably true that in no way can any parent gain such power of his child for the shaping of the child's character and habits of life as by having and showing sympathy with that child.... How many parents there are...who are readier to provide playthings for their children than to share the delights of their children with those playthings; readier to set their children at knowledge-seeking, than to have a part in their children's surprises and enjoyments of knowledge-attaining; readier to make good, as far as they can, all losses to their children, than to grieve with their children over those losses. And what a loss of power to those parents as parents, is this lack of sympathy with their children as children.[2]

If Trumbull had been the only author saying these things, I would have dismissed his argument, but I kept running into others saying the same thing. J. C. Ryle, a noted Anglican bishop and author, had this to say:

> Kindness, gentleness, long-suffering, forbearance, patience, sympathy, a willingness to enter into childish troubles, a readiness to take part in childish joys,—these are the cords by which a child may be led most easily,—these are the clues you must follow if you would find the way to his heart.[3]

And there were many others, all noted pastors and authors, and every one of them testifying to the power of parental sympathy. Here was a concept that seemed at one time to be a defining idea in childhood discipline, but after a century of changing values it seems to have disappeared.

SYMPATHY VERSUS STRICTNESS

In order to offer a biblical view of sympathy, I will first explain what it is not. Sympathy is not permissiveness or a parental softness that "lets children be children" with a disregard for their need for restraint or correction. Nor is sympathy pity, like the old ladies clucking their tongues and saying, "Such a pity. The poor lad just can't help himself."

The permissive discipline movement that began in the early fifties is still alive in spirit, if not in name. Thankfully, beginning in the seventies, Christian parents started to find solid ground with the "tough love" discipline messages of James Dobson and others. In the process, though, it seems we discarded the virtue of sympathy as we reacted against the philosophy of permissive discipline. We'll do ourselves and our children a great favor if we reclaim the Victorian-era meaning of sympathy and apply it in our families.

Sympathy, very simply, is "feeling with" another person.[4] But don't confuse sympathy with empathy. Empathy is closer to the idea of actually feeling what another is feeling, of entering into their emotions. In contrast, sympathy is not about feeling the same emotions your child feels, but rather understanding what your child is feeling and thinking. It is more like coming alongside your children as they process their own thoughts and feelings. That is what Jesus did when He observed the multitudes who were "distressed and dispirited like sheep without a shepherd" (Matthew 9:36). He had compassion for them; He was sympathetic.

In contrast with the sympathetic parent is the strict disciplinarian. The image that comes to mind is the parent who controls her child's behavior, punishing disobedience whenever it surfaces and tolerating no challenges to her authority. The rightness of strict discipline is widely accepted among Christian parents, and yet it has no real biblical basis.[5] My guess is that the widespread acceptance of the idea of strict discipline originates with the "spare the rod, spoil the child" axiom and the misapplication to young children of the Proverbs passages about the rod.

Strictness in discipline emphasizes the parent as the controlling party and puts parents in an adversarial role with their children. Exercised as a quick way to stop unwanted behavior, strictness as a guiding principle can easily become an expression of parental power rather than parental love. From the child's vantage point, adherence to the parent's exertion of power is based on the fear of further punishment rather than a heartfelt desire to please the parent.

Contrast that with the exercise of sympathy. Sympathy as a guiding attitude in discipline attempts to put parents in the role of advocate, enabling them to lead the child with love rather than with fear. Sympathy also desires to stop unwanted behavior, but it takes the time to look past the child's behavior to his heart. It asks, "What prompted my child's misbehavior, and how can I address the cause?"

PUTTING ON SYMPATHY

If you asked my children, they would agree that I'm not naturally the sympathetic type. When I had a chance to play the role of a black-robed, scowling, growling Pharisee in a dramatic musical of the life of Christ, it was no real stretch for me to be in character. Being a sympathetic daddy, especially when it comes to disciplining my children, requires supernatural resources to overcome my natural tendencies, but that is what the Holy Spirit lives in my heart to do. And that, in essence, is what it means to put on a face of sympathy. In the same way that Paul says in Colossians that, in our relationships with others in the body of Christ, we are to "put on love," the following insights help me "put on" sympathy (see Colossians 3:12-15).

Always Discipline in the Spirit

The greatest challenge to my walking in the power of the Holy Spirit at home is when I need to discipline one of my children. If I get upset and discipline out of anger or frustration, my discipline is ineffective because it has ceased to be biblical. Paul told the Galatians, "Walk by the Spirit, and you will not carry out the desire of the flesh," which he went on to say includes enmities, strife, outbursts of anger, disputes, and dissensions (see Galatians 5:16-21). In contrast, he says, "If we live by the Spirit, let us also walk by the Spirit," the fruit of which includes love, peace, patience, kindness, gentleness, and self-control (see Galatians 5:22-25). Those are all qualities of a sympathetic parent.

Anger has no place in childhood discipline. As James teaches, "The anger of man does not achieve the righteousness of God" (1:20). If I want my children to respond with an open heart to my discipline, I dare not let anger control me. It will close their hearts to me *and* to the Holy Spirit. Paul reminded the Romans of God's "kindness and tolerance and patience," and that it is "the kindness of God [that] leads you to repentance" (2:4). God judges hearts that are hardened against Him, but He patiently disciplines and directs all who have open hearts. Parental sympathy reflects God's kindness, and it keeps my children's hearts soft and open to me and to Him.

If you want to offer your children sympathy that will help open their hearts to your directive discipline, you first must walk in the power of the Holy Spirit. It is a spiritual discipline to listen for the Spirit's voice, to confess any fleshly sins that may be characterizing your discipline, and to ask God to fill you with His Spirit (to control or to empower you). When you pray like that, you open your heart to God for the fruit of the Spirit to be obvious in your life. The power of the Holy Spirit will enable you to respond lovingly to your children, with self-control, so that the character of Christ will be evident in your words and actions.

Learn the Language of Sympathy

If you studied a foreign language in school, it's safe to say you probably have forgotten most of it because you haven't been speaking it. Most of us are in a similar spot when it comes to sympathy. There is a language to sympathy, but we don't use it all that much, so we have forgotten it. Moms are better at verbalizing sympathy than dads, if only because most women are more verbal than most men. Although sympathy is also expressed nonverbally through hugs, touches, and loving looks, it is the verbal expressions of sympathy that touch the heart and spirit of a child. I can show sympathy to my children, but I have, quite literally, had to learn the language of sympathy in order to know how to communicate it to them.

Interpersonal communication skills can be learned and mastered, but it takes practice. Effective communication means knowing how, through what you say and how you say it, to give your children freedom to express feelings, fears, disappointments, weird ideas, and even wrong thoughts. It means knowing how to communicate your own thoughts and feelings in a way that your children will understand. It means learning how to ask questions and give advice effectively without putting your children on the defensive or piling up more guilt. It means being able to pray with your children.

Faced with a frustrated child who is exhibiting a bad attitude or who has just exploded into an emotional meltdown, I find that my natural inclination is to say, "Get control!" and then move on. But sometimes my children need to know that I know they're having a tough time. That's when I need to express concern in a sympathetic way: "I'll bet that was really frustrating for you. It sure would be for me. I can remember getting upset about things like that when I was your age." There really is no effective sympathy unless it is expressed in language that is understood by your child.

In their book *The Five Love Languages of Children,* Gary Chapman and Ross Campbell assert, "For a child to feel love, we must learn to speak her unique love language. Every child has a special way of perceiving love.... If you have several children in your family, chances are they speak different languages, for just as children often have different personalities, they may hear in different love languages."[6] Learning those love languages is learning the language of sympathy.

Know Your Child's Unique Personality

This next point is so obvious that it sounds odd to state it: You can't show sympathy unless you first really know your child. Each child's personality is from God. It has been programmed into his personal hard drive before he makes his entrance into the world.

Only God knows how many kinds of personalities He has made, so why would we ever think there is a one-size-fits-all way to relate to children? Just as God has given specific kinds of gifted people to the church in order to do ministry, He has also created specific kinds of personalities. Admittedly, there is no biblical model for personalities as there is for spiritual gifts, but sanctified observation reveals certain personality patterns.

Among my four children, I've found one each of four major types: a

Doer (one who gets things done and makes things work), a *Helper* (one who likes to help and who appreciates others), a *Mover* (one who lives to influence others to do great things), and a *Shaper* (one who is an architect of new ideas, concepts, and ways of doing things).[7] Some children are reflective or introverted (focusing their attention on thoughts and ideas); some are active or extroverted (focusing their attention on people and activities). Some are experience-oriented (needing freedom and spontaneity, while others are time-oriented (needing structure and predictability). But each child is unique. And the utter uniqueness of each child is essential to keep in mind when showing the face of sympathy. What communicates sympathy to one child may not do so to another.

Every personality type, however many there are, is designed by God. There is no grading of personality, with one style designated as "more spiritual" than another. Each personality has its own set of strengths and weaknesses, and each is wired differently when it comes to receiving input, care, and discipline. What that means for sympathetic discipline is that I can't treat every child the same way because each one will respond differently. To be a truly sympathetic parent, I need to understand each child's personality so I can know best how to reach that child's heart.

Discern Your Child's Real Needs

It always breaks my heart to see a strict mother harshly correcting an obviously exhausted young child. Both mother and child are being pushed to their limits, and as the situation worsens, the mother demands that the tired child behave *immediately* or face sure punishment. She offers no sympathy at all. I want to go pick up the child, speak softly to him, and comfort him. He doesn't need discipline; he needs a nap.

I'm embarrassed to think of how many times as a young parent I presented that kind of unsympathetic face to one of my children. I expected them to behave, no excuses allowed. Thankfully, God changed my thinking before I continued to inflict the mistake. As a more sympathetic parent, I now take the time to be sure my children actually need discipline. Much of the time, what they really need is rest, good food, or time to regroup. Children typically don't get enough rest in our busy culture, and tired children are not going to be as responsive to their parents. Similarly, if children have been playing hard all day, physical exhaustion will affect their attitudes. Being around lots of other children, especially in the younger years, will overstimulate kids and sometimes make them hyper. Hunger can create irritability. Too much of the wrong foods (such as sugar) can also affect temperament, and medication can have mood-altering effects. If I'm not looking for my children's real needs, I can end up disciplining the effects but not really addressing the cause. Sympathetic parents are aware of their children's real needs.

Spiritual and emotional needs also can affect behavior. If children are struggling with spiritual issues or fears, they may act them out or become withdrawn. They may not have the words they need to talk about what they're feeling, so they have no way to deal with the anxiety that results. Some children will quietly endure being teased about their weight, their looks, or their intellect, but their wounded hearts will affect their attitudes and behaviors until a wise parent can draw them out. Some children may need more emotional maintenance than others and will behave inappropriately when their "emotional tanks" run too low. In all these cases, if we are not addressing the real needs in our children's lives, we'll end up disciplining symptoms instead of the true cause.

Recently, a bee stung Joy, my younger daughter, on the lip. After the initial sting was gone, she seemed fine, so we gave her a dose of Benadryl and let her keep playing. A couple of hours later, she was acting irritable, talking back, and arguing. She angrily insisted that she wasn't tired and didn't need a nap. A strict parent might have rebuked her bad attitude and sent her to her room. Sally, though, said gently, "Joy, can I come and lie down with you for a few minutes? I just want to be with my sweet girl." When Joy was on the bed and calmed down, she said, "You know,

Mommy, sometimes I get so tired that I just can't seem to behave." That tired, physically hurting, medicated child needed sympathy, not correction.

SYMPATHY AND THE PATH OF LIFE

As you walk the path of life with your children, they need to know that you'll be with them. We tend to forget that, for children, life is a scary journey. I can remember as a young child feeling alone in my fears and uncertainties. That's why I have many times lain in bed with one of my children who was struggling with fearful thoughts. Sometimes we'd talk about what was bothering her, or about life, and sometimes I would just be there. My presence was a source of security in a time of insecurity. God the Father does this same thing for us: "In the fear of the LORD there is strong confidence, and his children will have refuge" (Proverbs 14:26). Your child needs to know that you will listen, understand, and put your arm around her as you walk the path of life together. Strictness and harshness will leave a child feeling alone, separated from you. Strictness demands obedience first; understanding is optional. Sympathy seeks understanding and expects obedience. The strict parent walks out front on the path and requires the child to follow, probably running to keep up with the parent's longer stride. But the sympathetic parent walks alongside a child and guides her.

Heartfelt discipline means accompanying children along the path of life, extending sympathy as you go. Essential to that journey is knowing that God created your children's hearts to be open to your guidance. Your children naturally want to walk alongside you because they know you want the best for them. As you provide the guidance your children need, their hearts will be further opened to you by the sympathy you offer them.

CHAPTER 6

ENCOURAGEMENT
VERSUS GUILT

The Power of Believing and Affirming

I don't know a parent who doesn't struggle with how to motivate his or her kids. How do I get my son or daughter to finish homework, to complete household chores, to obey, to do what is right? It shouldn't surprise us that Scripture presents an effective approach to motivating human behavior, and it does so through pairs of contrasting forces: the reward of heaven or the torment of hell, blessing or cursing, the path of life or the way of death. These external stimuli or promised outcomes provide incentive.

Love is the ultimate motivation we find in the New Testament, but it's not an external stimulus. Love is an internal motivation that prompts us to want to seek the rewards of obedience. Paul spoke of being "controlled" by love in his effort to persuade the Corinthian believers to choose to obediently follow Christ (see 2 Corinthians 5:14). In a similar way, it is sympathy, an expression of that love, that orients your children's hearts to your efforts to lead them along the path of life. As you lead them, you want to motivate them to say yes to righteousness and no to unrighteousness—to choose wisdom over foolishness, God's ways over the world's, right instead of wrong. How you motivate them to make those choices will have a lasting impact on how your children view God.

Unfortunately, motivating by guilt or fear comes much more naturally.

In the rush of daily life, we're probably not even aware when we're using guilt. It's quicker and more efficient simply to correct children and tell them why they should feel bad about their misbehavior: "I can't believe you did that. That was pretty foolish, wasn't it? You know better than that."

Paul talked about creating a "godly sorrow" that leads to repentance (see 2 Corinthians 7:8-11), but that is different from shame. Godly sorrow is a true conviction of sin that turns a person back to God. Inadvertently, we parents can use words that we think are causing our children to feel bad about their sin (godly sorrow) but in reality are causing them to feel bad about themselves (guilt and shame). Doing the relational work of directive discipline instead seems much more inconvenient and time-consuming.

Think back to your own childhood. What motivated you to want to do good? Was it the negative messages: "When are you going to grow up and take more responsibility? You're old enough to do this on your own!" Or was it the positive messages of encouragement that pointed to what you were becoming: "I know you can do better because I see what God is doing in your life. I want to help you learn how to be more responsible, so here's what I want us to do." Even words as simple as "Stop acting like a child" can communicate a sense of guilt and shame. Children should never have to feel bad about being childish—what else *can* they be? The reality is this: Making our children feel bad about themselves will not make them more mature.

The English word *encouragement* means to instill courage or boldness into another person. In contrast, *discourage* means to remove courage, leaving in its place fear or resignation. Encouragement in discipline means giving your children the courage or strength to do or be what is right. You're helping them grow in maturity. By its nature, guilt discourages children because it's based on shame and fear. Guilt can't lead to maturity because, according to John, "There is no fear in love; but perfect love casts out fear, because fear involves punishment, and the one who fears is not perfected in love" (1 John 4:18). Encouragement is an expression of love that will

help your children be "perfected," which is a Greek word that is also translated "mature."

The Greek word translated "encouragement" in the New Testament is
parakaleo. It is a compound of *para,* "alongside," and *kaleo,* "to call." It pictures someone who comes alongside to help and to comfort. In John 14,
Jesus told His disciples that, when He returned to the Father, He would
send them another Helper *(paraclete),* the Holy Spirit, who would be with
them in His place. However, in numerous other places, *parakaleo* is translated to mean "encouragement." Applied to heartfelt discipline, this reality
of being called alongside offers a vivid picture of your role in the life of your
children. You come alongside to provide needed help. In a sense, you are a
representative of the Holy Spirit in your children's lives to help them
become mature. That is why it's so critical that you understand the necessity of walking in the power of the Spirit as you discipline your children.

THE FACE OF ENCOURAGEMENT

Directive discipline is so named because it helps you direct your child's
heart to want to walk God's path of life with you. It is based in relationship, in a sharing of hearts. Encouragement is an expression of love that will
foster that relationship. When you put on a face of encouragement for your
children, you find ways to let them know you believe in them, that they
are important to God, and that you recognize and affirm the good character traits you're seeing in their lives. Guilt, on the other hand, simply judges
and condemns, and ultimately it separates. It is impossible to use guilt to
encourage a child.

As you consider offering encouragement or guilt, realize that your
words and attitudes will have a lifelong impact on your children's hearts.
During your children's formative years, your words of encouragement will
not only be a strong motivator for them to follow God, but your affirming

words will also strengthen your relationship with them and keep their emotional tank filled with love.

True encouragement is not flattery about external looks or dress or abilities, nor is it the feel-good pep-talk of some self-esteem programs. And I'm not talking about just saying nice things to your child, even though good words will add to the nurturing environment in your home. I'm talking about biblical encouragement as a divine mandate. Believers are admonished to "encourage one another day after day" so that we won't become "hardened by the deceitfulness of sin" (Hebrews 3:13). Your children need biblical encouragement.

Every day, your children are exposed to a barrage of secular messages and images that seek to sway their allegiances. Studies have shown that most high-school seniors no longer believe in moral absolutes. They have heard the message of moral relativism since childhood, so why should they? Christian schools and homeschooling can mitigate that influence, but don't be fooled into believing either can eliminate it. Secularism is pervasive and aggressive, and it is targeted more and more at children.[1]

Although you'll need to find an age-appropriate, child-friendly format, you need to encourage your children to "continue in the faith" (Acts 14:22), to resist sin, and to resist the things that would draw them away from God. As a member of Christ's family, you are the source for that biblical encouragement for your children (see Hebrews 3:13). Biblical encouragement is part of directive discipline that will help keep your child walking on the path of life.

Encourage Your Children Daily

Most of the day-to-day activities we do with our children require little forethought or planning. They are the habits, rituals, and routines of family life. Biblical encouragement, though, must be consciously and purposefully cultivated. Even a daily devotional or family time can become rote and lose the element of true biblical encouragement. But children vitally need the affirmation and encouragement that come through a parent's thoughtful application of biblical truth to their individual lives. I'm talking about not just a prayer as your children leave the house, but a word from you that you have received from God to implant in their hearts and minds.

And you cannot offer a word from God unless you have spent time with Him. Scripture is full of examples of seeking God daily. One of my favorites in Psalm 1, in which the "blessed man" is the one whose "delight is in the law of the LORD, and in His law he meditates day and night" (Psalm 1:2). Because it was chosen to be the first psalm, this idea is elevated and emphasized. Of course, parents are instructed in Deuteronomy 6:4-9 to talk about God's truth "when you lie down and when you rise up," an idiomatic way of saying all the time, but this passage also emphasizes the daily need to encourage our children in their faith. In the New Testament, the young church met "every day" (Acts 2:46, NIV), and the writer of Hebrews admonishes Christians to "encourage one another day after day" (3:13).

As I write these words, I am convicted of my need to daily encourage my children in the faith. I have an eighteen-year-old daughter who needs the encouragement of God's Word to be faithful in her choices. I have thirteen- and sixteen-year-old boys who are charging through the time of young manhood when their beliefs and values will be set for a lifetime. I need more than ever, every day, to encourage them from the Word in order to help them stand strong against temptation to sin and to keep their feet on God's path of life. I have a seven-year-old daughter blossoming into childhood who needs her daddy to give her words of encouragement that will set her heart thinking about the God her mother and I love and follow. It isn't enough for me to do this kind of encouraging every now and then; I need to do it every day for each of my children. It's a discipline of maturity and parenthood that I must choose to develop.

Encourage Your Children from God's Word

Encouragement can take many forms, but it isn't biblical encouragement without the Word of God at its heart. Perhaps an actual Scripture reading or recitation is the best thing because then your children hear and are encouraged by God's own words. However, there is more to biblical encouragement than quotes direct from Scripture. Much of Christian truth, such as the sermons of Jesus or John the Baptist, was transmitted orally at first, so it wasn't always a verbatim quotation of scriptural text that was shared. Encouragement may be a scripture read or quoted, but it also can be a generalized biblical truth or wisdom principle, a condensed story from the Bible, or a paraphrased parable of Jesus.

That said, Scripture that is read or recited from memory is the purest form of biblical encouragement. As you use the Bible to encourage your children, you are relying on the Holy Spirit to direct your words and God's Word to them. You may be thinking, *But I don't know what to say. That's why I need to read from a devotional book.* But the same Holy Spirit that Jesus promised His disciples, of whom He said, "He will guide you into all the truth," is the Spirit who lives and works in your heart (John 16:13). If you ask the Holy Spirit to give you something to say to your children, He will. It doesn't matter if your message is ten words of Scripture or ten thousand. If you offer it in the power of the Spirit, it will be effective.

Let's say I'm reading the Bible and Matthew 6:33 speaks to my heart: "But seek first His kingdom and His righteousness, and all these things will be added to you." This verse might prompt me to pray that each of my children will come to understand what it means to seek God's kingdom. Later, I might be talking with one of my children and share something like this: "I prayed for you this morning. I read the Scripture that says, 'But seek first His Kingdom and His righteousness, and all these things will be added to you.' Did you know that you can't see God's kingdom with your eyes? It's not made of land and castles, but of people. You have to seek it to see it because it's in your heart. This morning, I prayed that when you seek

God's kingdom, you will see it, just as I have." This is just a brief bit of encouragement, but because it came from the Spirit of God and spoke the Word of God, it will be effective (see Isaiah 55:11).

Encourage Your Children in Order to Give Them Hope

There is a verse of Scripture that puts *courage* into encouragement. In Romans 14–15, Paul wrote about the weak and the strong in the church and about our responsibility to build up one another and to be unified in our faith. Paul's statement in 15:4 gets to the heart of why we must encourage our children: "For whatever was written in earlier times was written for our instruction, so that through perseverance and the encouragement of the Scriptures we might have hope." God gave us the Scriptures to teach us the things that enable us to continue in the faith and to encourage us so that we might have hope. The Scriptures help us walk the path of life with confidence. Our children need this same hope and confidence.

How often have you thought, *I need to be sure my child has hope!* Probably not very often. In our culture, childhood is considered a time of innocence and wonder, a season of smiles and laughter that needs protection from life's hard issues. We don't naturally think that there could be a place of despair in a precious child's heart. But I know that children have these feelings because I did when I was young.

At one time I sat alone in my room, pondering the imponderables of life, contemplating eternity and infinity. I can still feel the force of despair and fear that swept over my spirit when I realized what I was thinking. There was a reality that did not end, that was not bound by the laws of time and the cycle of birth and death, beginning and end. There was a realm out there that was completely foreign to my daily life and experience, and I didn't know what to do about it. It was a terrifying thought. I didn't share those thoughts with anyone, and no one drew them out of me. They remained a place of despair in my heart for many years until I began to hear the truth about God.

Your children need you to give them the encouragement of the Scriptures that will provide hope. Children's lives are full of questions and confusion. They need hope, and Paul taught that the Scriptures were written for that very purpose.

But how do the Scriptures give a child hope? Jeremiah the prophet had an answer: It is because God's Word reveals to us the faithfulness of God in the lives of people and nations. "This I recall to mind, therefore I have hope. The LORD's lovingkindnesses indeed never cease, for His compassions never fail. They are new every morning; great is Your faithfulness" (Lamentations 3:21-23). When a child sees that God has been real to generation after generation of those who believe in Him and that He has been faithful to His followers without fail, then that child can also believe that God is real and will be faithful to him. And in that truth he will find hope.

So show your children the faithfulness of God in history—how the prophecies and promises of God are true and were fulfilled hundreds of years after being given. Show them God's faithfulness in your own life— how He is faithful to your family. Every year we have a Family Day when we review all the ways God was faithful to us in the prior year. We make a list of God's acts of faithfulness and divvy it up. Then every family member draws pictures that depict God's loving acts. It's a poignant and visual reminder to our children that, no matter what happens, God is faithful. These are our memorial stones of remembrance, hand-drawn pictures kept in a notebook, like the stones Joshua made into a memorial when Israel crossed the Jordan into the Promised Land. Back then, fathers were to point to these memorials to remind their children of God's faithfulness. The direct encouragement of the Scriptures will give our children hope and a reason to be faithful.

Affirm Your Children's Strengths and Potential

Making your words personal is key to effectively encouraging your children. When you apply a scripture to your child's life, choose one that speaks to a need she feels, to something she has experienced, or to a hope or dream she has shared. As you do so, you are giving your child a vicarious experience of mature, Christian faith-thinking. Your ten-year-old may not have the vocabulary to express deep insights about God and life, but she is able to understand and imagine much more than she can put into words. When you personalize Scripture for her, you are helping her recognize what's in her heart, but what she is not yet able to articulate. This is critical to giving your child the words and ways of Christianity in advance of the time that she makes a personal commitment to Christ. This is preparation for the moment when Christ will give your child a new spirit.

To personalize Scripture in our home, we've made it a practice not to say, "I wonder what you'll do when you grow up." Instead, we say, "I know what you will do! You'll serve God with your life as He expands His kingdom in this world. Now, I wonder what your role in God's plan will be." Sarah, my older daughter, has always enjoyed writing. So our personalized encouragement for her might be: "Sarah, God has given you a special ability to communicate His truth to others. I'm going to pray that God will show you how to invest your talents for His glory." Joel, my older son, is drawn to playing the guitar and writing songs. Personalized encouragement for him might be: "Joel, I love to hear you play your guitar. It reminds me that God has made each of us creative in a special way. I can really see the image of God in your life through your music. Can you imagine yourself leading others in worship?"

Personalizing your encouragement communicates to your children that you are looking not just at what they do, but also at who they are. You are identifying how God is working in their lives and envisioning how He can use them now as well as in the future.

Acknowledge Good Choices and Actions

Be sure to catch your children doing good, and when you do, encourage them. Share with them from Scripture why their choice pleases God, how it is an expression of godly virtue or character, or how it shows that they are becoming more mature. Biblical encouragement comes not just from affirming good behavior, but from connecting it with a scriptural truth. Doing so helps your children begin to see that their lives are connected to God.

For most children, negative thoughts and feelings associated with being corrected, no matter how lovingly the correction is given, stick with them. And there is a cumulative effect when children are corrected often. Most research indicates that it takes several positive messages to offset the impact of just one negative message. So make it a point to acknowledge your children's good choices and behavior. It's our natural tendency not to affirm good behavior, perhaps assuming that our children should be behaving anyway and that obedience should not warrant special recognition. But our children need the encouragement that comes from our affirmation that they are growing more mature, even if just a little every day.

Paul reminded us that "God demonstrates His own love toward us, in that while we were yet sinners, Christ died for us" (Romans 5:8). God didn't wait for us to get it all right. Instead He saw something in us worth redeeming because we are stamped with His image. His love looked past our sin to see our potential in Christ. As parents, we are called to love our children that way, to express our belief in them and in what they can become despite their sin, and to see God at work in them before they see it themselves.

Add Some Humor and Laughter to the Mix

Finally, as you affirm and encourage your children, remember to maintain some lightness in your conversations. You don't have to be Bill Cosby to add a light touch to your words of encouragement. A wisecrack here, a bad pun there, a play on words, or a humorous observation all get a laugh. Even if you have trouble remembering jokes, you can still add a touch of humor to your conversations.

This is important because children like to laugh. We all do. It's a form of encouragement that can lighten the spirit. As a wise man long ago observed, "A joyful heart is good medicine" (Proverbs 17:22). After all, it was God's idea to create us with a sense of humor, to make us people who can laugh, so it must be good if the reason for laughter is good. Adding some smiles and humor to your encouragement, when it's appropriate, will make your words a bit more effective and a lot more fun. In our scary and serious world, your children need the kind of encouragement that comes with laughter. So lighten up every now and then and make merry.

ENCOURAGEMENT ALONG THE PATH OF LIFE

Imagine hiking a mountain trail for the first time. Since you've never before been in this terrain, you're unfamiliar not only with the weight of the backpack, the clumsy hiking boots, and the thin air, but you're also a bit apprehensive because you know the trail will have some steep and rocky sections. At the same time, you know you'll be hiking with an experienced trail guide, so you can relax a bit and think about the beautiful scenery you'll enjoy along the way. That is, until you get on the trail.

As you struggle over difficult stretches of the trail and try to negotiate steep, rocky slopes, your guide glances back with an occasional "keep going" look and a smile. But he always lets you know when you've done something the wrong way. He talks about what trails are like and about his experiences on various trails, and he's very nice and communicative, but you feel alone and like you'll never get it right. With blisters burning your feet and with leg and back muscles weary and aching, it's little wonder that you're now discouraged.

I'm afraid parents are often like that trail guide. What's missing from the parenting process is the simple practice of encouragement. Your children are on a journey along God's path of life, and God has assigned you to be the trail guide. You already know how to walk the path, but your children don't. While they need instruction and correction in order to walk the path well, they also need your encouragement. They need to hear why it's important for them to walk this path, that they are walking it well, and that they, too, will one day be great trail guides for their own children and for others. Coming alongside your children as you walk the path together, and being an encourager along the way, may be the most important things you ever do for them.

NURTURE VERSUS NEGLECT

The Power of Perceiving and Helping

We all know what happens to a child who is physically neglected. We see it all the time in ads seeking financial contributions to help feed children in Third World countries. Their emaciated bodies and sunken eyes make them seem completely lost and without hope. But neglect isn't just about food. We also see children in our own communities who are starving for love or even just for some caring parental involvement. They, too, are undernourished. They are emotionally emaciated, and they seem lost and without hope. Both groups of children need to be nurtured.

When you hear the word *nurture,* you're likely to imagine a mother with her children, perhaps with a baby at her breast. It's a warm, relational word that suggests the giving of life. You might not associate nurture with older children or young adults, much less with adults. And nurture may not seem like a legitimate component of discipline. But a closer look at Scripture gives us a different perspective.

Three words with meanings associated with *nurture* are used in the New Testament. Two of the words describe nursing, feeding, and being brought up. A third form of the word, though, is used in only two places, both times in the book of Ephesians. Paul made a point in Ephesians 5:29 that husbands should love their wives in the same way they love their own bodies, "for no one ever hated his own flesh, but *nourishes* and cherishes it, just as Christ also does the church." Paul painted a picture of a husband as nourishing, or nurturing, his wife. The term he used is *ektrepho,* which means, literally, "to feed from." The idea is that a husband's nurture is an act of caring for his wife, treating her spirit as a living thing that needs special attention. Today, we might call it TLC (tender loving care). You may wonder what that has to do with childhood discipline. Keep reading.

In Ephesians 6:4, Paul addressed the same men, instructing those who are parents: "Fathers, do not provoke your children to anger, but *bring them up* in the discipline and instruction of the Lord." The Greek work for "bring them up" is the same word Paul used for "nourish" just eight verses earlier. In the same way that husbands are to nurture the lives of their wives, fathers are to nurture the lives of their children. Paul added that this nurture is to include both discipline and instruction, but don't lose the impact of the word. Fathers (not just nursing or tender mothers) are to be nurturing, are to see their children as living beings who need to be fed in order to grow and develop. Nurture of children is not an option, it's a command (see Ephesians 6:4), and it is directly associated with the larger picture of discipline.

When we see a child who is physically or emotionally deprived, our hearts break because we know that the neglect will affect that child for the rest of his life. I'm not talking about abuse, but simple neglect. We have trouble understanding how parents could neglect their child's needs for food or basic care. But what about neglect at the spiritual level? We would never think of withholding nourishing food or warm hugs from our children, but are we ever guilty of benign neglect of their spiritual needs?

When Paul wrote, "Bring them up in the discipline and instruction of the Lord" (Ephesians 6:4), I believe there's more to his language than simply "raise your children to be Christians." He was calling parents to an active, involved, nurturing role. A Christian home is not defined by kids never missing Sunday school and Bible club, listening only to Christian music, watching Christian videos, and memorizing lots of Bible verses. A Christian home is never defined by what the *children* do. It's defined by what the *parents* do. Only you can create a Christian home by being a nurturing parent in the fullest sense of the word.

True biblical nurture means bringing the reality of Christ into your child's life through your life at home. The simple biblical truth is that there is no "life" apart from Christ. He is "the way, and the truth, and the *life*" (John 14:6), and while our children are young, it is our responsibility to make that life a reality to them. It's a critical part of preparing their spirits to receive the seed of the Word of God. You make plans to feed your children nutritious meals so they will have strong physical lives; you make sure they are safe, secure, and loved so they will have strong emotional lives; and you need to make sure they are tasting the reality of Christ in your home so they will have strong spiritual lives. We dare not neglect this spiritual nurture.

Spiritually nurturing your children involves preparing the soil of their spirits so the Word of God can take root there. Like cultivating a garden, the process requires thinking and planning. You would never plant vegetable seeds and then just expect them to grow because you put them in the ground. You would plan what you needed to do to make the garden grow, when to pull the weeds, and when to water the plants, and you would stick to that plan religiously knowing that the survival of your seedlings would be in danger if you did not. Keep that same picture in mind regarding your children.

Think and plan ahead about how to make spiritual nurture a part of your daily life. Here are some practical actions you can take to nurture the life of Christ in your children.

SPEND TIME TOGETHER AS A FAMILY

To really nurture your children, you may have to live counterculturally. Put differently, you might have to take a step away from culture to reclaim your nurturing role. Even within the Christian culture, we have substituted lifestage activities for family togetherness. That's nowhere more evident than on Sunday morning when the average family goes in five different directions as soon as they arrive at church. The rest of the week, calendar-filling church events, children's ministries, youth groups, sports, school activities, concerts, small groups, and myriad other events all keep families from being together.

In contrast, one of the hallmark characteristics of Jesus' ministry is that His disciples were with Him. If you think about it, three years wasn't a long time for Him to prepare eleven of His twelve closest followers to establish the church. But it was three years of being with Jesus—of talking with Him every day, listening to His teaching, watching His miracles, feeling His embrace—that made that time long enough. You have a lot longer than three years to spend with each of your children, but that may not be long enough if they are seldom with you. If culture gets more of your children than you do, then it's time to reclaim your God-given nurturing role in their lives.

You can start with the simple choices. First, cut out nonessential activities. If you take a hard look at your calendar, it's not that difficult to start doing less. So, with input from your children, determine to limit their activities. Think of it this way: Sun is needed to grow plants, but too much sun will cause them to wither and dry up. Activity is good, but too many activities, especially at the cost of time with the family, will leave your children depleted and dried up spiritually. Reclaim some of the hours that have been sacrificed on the altar of the false god of activity and give those hours back to God. Consider them as holy moments in your week when you're going to bring the presence of God into your family.

Next, you need to sanctify the time you reclaim, to set it apart for God's use. Plan a family night that includes a fun meal together, some family games or activities, and some time to talk about God's Word. Make the time around the Bible creative, interactive, and interesting. Have an inspirational video/DVD night, including a time to talk about the movie and to look up some scriptures over a fun dessert. Have a read-aloud book night where everyone shares in the reading, or listen to an inspiring book on tape. Be creative about bringing the reality of God's presence into whatever you're doing.

Finally, always be thinking about how to involve your children in what you are doing. When Sally and I have speaking engagements or ministry trips, we always try to take one or more of our kids with us. Let your children see your life up close so they can see God at work there. Let your children experience ministry with you so they can sense God's reality in their own family. It's the Deuteronomy 6:4-9 principle of sharing God's truth with your children "when you sit in your house and when you walk by the way." No matter where you are or what you are doing, your children should hear God's truth from you.

MAKE FAMILY DEVOTIONS A PRIORITY

In a busy culture, this discipline can be difficult to maintain, but it's critical for the spiritual health of your children. The writer of Psalm 1 highlighted meditating on God's Word "day and night" (verse 2). Morning and evening meditations were common among the Jews, and believers practiced this in order to stay on God's path of righteousness. Things haven't changed much since then. We still need regular, daily input from God if we are to live fruitful lives, and our children need both to see us turning to God each day and experience it with us. Unlike the psalmist, who didn't have a neatly bound copy of the holy writings at home, we are awash in Bibles, but we must open and read them if we are to experience God's reality. A simple, regular family devotional time is the starting place. It doesn't matter if it's morning or evening or both, as long as it's regular.

In the same way that we are awash in Bibles, we also have access to dozens of devotional resources. As I have reviewed many of them for our ministry Web-site bookstore, I've realized that very few are serious about making God real. Too many try hard to be culturally relevant and end up being contrived, silly, or pedantic. Others are just too simplistic, childish, and shallow to be of much use. But there are a few serious, creative, well-written, thoughtful devotionals for families who really want to know God. So use discernment when choosing a devotional guide. At the same time, be cautious about becoming dependent on devotionals. Don't fall into the trap of believing that you can't lead family devotions without a guide. Since the Word of God is true, it's all you really need.

If you feel nervous about a Bible-only approach to devotions, try the Family Devotional ARTS approach. Using this simple method, any parent can lead a meaningful devotional time with a Bible and little or no preparation. To follow is the basic outline.

A—Ask a Question

Once you find a passage you want to discuss, think of a fun question to ask that will pique your children's interest. For example, if you're reading about David and Goliath, ask, "What would it be like if you grew up to be nine feet tall?" Let that generate some discussion and laughter. The initial question can be imaginative, and it should be open-ended, asking for opinions rather than a right answer.

R—Read the Bible

Read your Bible text out loud. When you read, do it slowly and expressively. We tend to read the Bible too fast, especially for children, and without emotion. Any portion of Scripture—history, wisdom, prophecy, parable, teaching—can be read with expression. The Bible is "living and active" (Hebrews 4:12), but we can make it deadly and dull by how we read its words of life.

T—Talk About It

Next, ask questions about the text that get at the content and spiritual lessons of the passage. Detail is important, but it's the spiritual insights that you want your children to discover. Ask what made David, a boy, so brave as he faced Goliath. Ask what sin brought Goliath's destruction. Ask about the kinds of giants that we have to face today.

S—Speak to God

Finally, speak to God about the lesson. Most devotionals seem to make application the final stage, adding some activity to do during the day (that never really gets done). The most important application for your children is to apply the lesson through prayer. Suggest some ways they can pray: "Give me courage and faith like David. Help me never to be prideful like Goliath." It is by those prayers—by asking God into their days—that they will experience more fully the reality of God in their lives.[1]

MAKE FAMILY TRADITIONS SPIRITUALLY MEANINGFUL

The next step, along with time together and regular family devotions, is to bring the reality of God into your family traditions and holidays. Those times are full of fun and good memories, but for many Christian families they are celebrations pretty much divorced from God. Many of the special days that could be spiritual anchors in your children's lives and hearts have had the spiritual content either secularized or commercialized right out of them. When you add the spiritual content back in, and take it further by showing the meaning, you are injecting spiritual life into those special times.

Just for the record, holidays were God's idea. He created several for the Jews who apparently liked the idea so much that they created others. These were never simply recreational days as our holidays have become; they were first and foremost educational. Christianity has followed the same pattern in creating holidays around key biblical events. Christmas and Easter have no biblical mandate, but they are patterned after God's use of holidays to commemorate His actions in history and in our lives. God is never opposed to traditions except when they become empty observances that serve no purpose for Him or require adherence to man-made rules over God's requirements. When holidays and traditions reflect His reality, then God is honored (see Romans 14:5-6; Colossians 2:16-17).

If your holidays and traditions have become dead in the sense that there is no life of God in them, then it's time to reclaim them for Him. These special days can be powerful anchors in your children's lives, acting as touchstones for important aspects of their childhood. If you are serious about nurturing your children with God's reality, then you must become serious about reviving your holiday celebrations. Here are a few simple ideas to get you started.

Christmas

An advent wreath is an easy way to focus on Christ during the holiday season. The four Sundays before Christmas and Christmas Eve become times when you light the candles, read scriptures, and talk about the meaning and significance of the incarnation of Christ.

On Christmas Eve, my family also has a Shepherd's Meal. Sally serves herb bread, cheeses, soups, nuts, and juices—a simple meal like the shepherds may have eaten. Then we read, and sometimes reenact, the Christmas story from Luke and sing Christmas hymns. In recent years, we have added a search for the baby Jesus (the figurine from our crèche) and the presenting of three gifts by each family member to Christ: a gift of service to another family member, a gift of commitment to God for personal growth, and a gift of money to a ministry or someone in need. A nice benefit is that having a meaningful Christmas Eve tradition means the children can enjoy Christmas morning with both stockings and gifts.

Easter—Resurrection Day

This holiday celebration should be the year's most meaningful, but it often gets lost among spring activities. Many families settle for an Easter church service and a big Easter dinner. With a little forethought, though, we can make the week of Christ's Passion a rich time of remembrance and reflection. This is the holiday, after all, that recalls the reason we have life in Christ: He died for our sins and then conquered death.

One easy way to increase the nurturing value of Holy Week is to read from the Scriptures each day about the events leading up to Christ's death and resurrection. On Palm Sunday—for just your family and friends—plan a celebrative fellowship meal with praise and testimonies. On Good Friday, plan a more reflective time of sharing, focusing on the words Christ spoke in the Upper Room or reviewing the Passion narrative, possibly celebrating Communion together and spending time in prayer. If you can, find a guidebook and have a Christian seder that will reveal the biblical and prophetic meaning of the elements of the Jewish Passover meal. It will be a powerful visual lesson for your children. Take some time Saturday night to talk to your children about sin, our need for a Savior, and the plan of salvation—they can never hear it enough. Then go to church Sunday morning and worship together as a family.

Thanksgiving

Use this holiday as an opportunity to talk about God's faithfulness and sovereignty in the affairs of history. It's a good time to give thanks, offer praise, and worship God together. Between the football games (or even instead of them), have a special time of worship and the giving of thanks with your own family or with other families.

Birthdays

For many years in my family, we have started the day with a birthday breakfast and family presents, then invited friends over that night for a birthday dinner. One of our special traditions is to go around the room and have each person either tell how they have seen the birthday person grow in the past year or offer an encouraging comment about that person. We might use Luke 2:52 as a model for talking about growth—intellectual, physical, spiritual, and social. Then we take time to pray for that person and for his or her growth in the year ahead.

An Opportunity with Every Holiday
Every holiday grounded in Christian history or events can be either an empty, dead celebration, or it can be infused with meaning by using it to bring the reality of God into your home. When you do that, and when it becomes a year-after-year tradition, you are providing a powerful ministry of nurture in your children's lives that will keep them walking on God's path of life.

MAKE THE WORD OF GOD
ACTIVE IN YOUR HOME

Making God real to your children doesn't stop with family nights, family devotions, and God-centered traditions. Remember that the Deuteronomy passage commands parents to teach God's truth to their children all the time and wherever they are. There really are no Bible-free zones in God's plan for nurturing children. The Word of God should intersect our lives at every point and place, especially when our children are present.

At this point we move from simple celebrations and routines into the more complex realm of dynamically living out our own faith relationship with God in front of our children. This is where we go from flying by instruments to flying by instinct. Moses told the parents of Israel, "These words, which I am commanding you today, shall be on your heart" (Deuteronomy 6:6). He was pointing out that they could not teach their children what was not already on their own hearts. In the same way, the truth of God must be on our hearts if we are to teach our children at any time and any place throughout the day.

The way to begin making God a part of every minute of your day is to meet with God daily. The more the Word of God permeates your own life and heart, the more you'll be able to bring God's Word into the lives of your children. I don't want to implicitly encourage a kind of trivializing of the Bible by making every incident during the day a Bible lesson. Rather, discussing God's truth is a natural outgrowth of having His Word on my heart. Your daily time in Scripture can open your eyes to a biblical principle that needs to be applied to a problem, to a verse that can enlighten a discussion, to biblical wisdom that will guide discipline or correction, to a passage that can be a prayer for a family need, or to a scripture about God's protection for a frightened child at bedtime.

There is no plan or schedule or resource that can provide this kind of nurture. It involves simply letting your children see in your life the truth of Psalm 119:105, that "Your word is a lamp to my feet and a light to my path." As you and your child walk the path of life together, the light of the reality of God in your life will nurture your child's spiritual life.

MAKE TIME EACH DAY FOR AFFECTION

Touch is associated more with physical nurture than with spiritual nurture, but you can't really separate the two. The idea of showing godly and appropriate affection is not addressed specifically by Scripture, but it is certainly inherent in the Bible's teaching. Biblical references to embraces, kisses, loving touches, healing touches, looks, expressions, considerate tone of voice, and more are sprinkled throughout Scripture. Paul often told believers to greet one another with a "holy kiss" (Romans 16:16; 1 Corinthians 16:20, 2 Corinthians 13:12; 1 Thessalonians 5:26), and Peter urged a "kiss of love" (1 Peter 5:14). We know by experience, even without a chapter and verse reference, that human beings need touch and appropriate affection. The biblical images of infants being cradled and children being held and protected leave little doubt that affection is as essential to the human condition as breathing. And wouldn't we all want to have been one of those children Jesus took in His arms, laid His hands on, and blessed (Mark 10:13-16)? His touch was as much a part of the blessing as His words.

Every family determines its own level of affection. Some families are quite verbally and physically affectionate; others are more restrained and less overt; while still others are light and casual. What is important, though, is to realize that affection and touch are part of our nurturing role. A hug with a verse of Scripture; sitting side-by-side to read a passage from the Bible; a touch on the arm or an arm around the shoulder when encouraging a child; a noogie on an uncombed head of hair—all of these create heart connections as you spiritually nurture your children with God's Word.

NURTURE ALONG THE PATH OF LIFE

Heartfelt discipline begins when you become a godly guide on the path of life. If the rest of your discipline—whether correction or protection—is to have any meaning, then your discipline of direction must infuse your children with the reality of the living God. That is the purpose of nurture.

In 1 Thessalonians 2:7-12, Paul described the way he and Silas related to the believers in that church. He used the language of a mother and father and in doing so revealed, I believe, his own view of God's design for parents. It is a rich portrait of spiritual nurture.

> But we proved to be *gentle* among you, *as a nursing mother tenderly cares for her own children.* Having so fond an *affection* for you, we were well-pleased to impart to you not only the gospel of God but also *our own lives,* because you had become *very dear* to us.... You

are witnesses, and so is God, how devoutly and uprightly and blamelessly we behaved toward you believers; just as you know how we were *exhorting and encouraging and imploring* each one of you *as a father would his own children,* so that you would walk in a manner worthy of the God who calls you into His own kingdom and glory.

The nurture that our children are designed to receive from us includes gentleness, tenderness, and affection infused with the reality of God and of His truth. Our exhorting, encouraging, and imploring is not about controlling behavior but about directing our children to "walk in a manner worthy of…God." It is about walking with them on the path of life. And that journey is the goal as well as the blessing of spiritual nurture.

INSTRUCTION VERSUS INFORMATION

The Power of Discernment and Godly Counsel

H ave you ever used the words "Because I said so, that's why!" when you needed to reprove or correct your child? That phrase, or something similar, has come out of my mouth more than once. As soon as I've said the words, though, I've known that I've uttered something that's not of the Spirit. Instead, I have simply used my parental power to close off debate. I "won," but it was too costly a victory. I lost the opportunity to offer the more important part of discipline—instruction in God's Word.

At other moments, when I've reproved one of my children in a carefully reasoned way, my words still haven't measured up. I would reprove them by carefully analyzing the incident, parsing all the words that caused conflict, separating the excuses from the bad attitudes, and offering some sound advice on how to avoid the situation in the future. We would part with smiles, but a nagging feeling of dissatisfaction would still be in my spirit. Why? Because I would know that the incident was all about *my* instruction, not *God's* instruction.

But then there are those times when I know I need to correct one of my children, and I do it right. Let's say one of my kids, in the midst of a disagreement with a sibling, has said mean things. This time, I ask God to give me wisdom and insight into the situation. I also ask Him to convict my child of sin and open my child's heart to instruction. As I respond to my child, I bring Scripture into the conversation, reminding him or her that anger is one of the deeds of the flesh, but that the fruit of God's Spirit is "love, joy, peace, patience, kindness, goodness, faithfulness, gentleness, self-control" (Galatians 5:22-23). I recall a proverb that says, "An angry man stirs up strife" (Proverbs 29:22), and share that Paul told the Colossians to put aside "anger, wrath, malice, slander, and abusive speech from your mouth" and to "put on" Christ (see 3:8,10). We look up the passage and see that it talks about "bearing with one another, and forgiving each other, whoever has a complaint against anyone; just as the Lord forgave you..." (Colossians 3:13). The conflict is eventually resolved, and forgiveness asked and received.

What made the difference? Only one thing—instruction from the Word of God. Rather than the focus being on what *I* had to say or on *my* reactions or insights, the focus was on what *God* had to say. The power of God's Word is undeniable. My words have no power to pierce my child's heart "as far as the division of soul and spirit, of both joints and marrow" and then to "judge the thoughts and intentions of the heart," but the "living and active" Word of God can do that (Hebrews 4:12). It is a "two-edged sword" that cuts through to the heart of every child and every situation, but, like any sword, it must be drawn and used. That is what the Bible calls instruction, and discipline is not biblical unless it includes biblical instruction.

Scripture does not view discipline as a series of isolated acts. The scriptural view encompasses the entire process of leading and influencing another person to choose and to walk in God's ways. The process of childhood discipline is best described as a parent serving as a godly guide as parent and child walk together on the path of life. As that guide, three priorities define parents' biblical responsibility to discipline their children: direction, correction, and protection. The first of these, direction, is a positive, loving expression that enables the parents to gain the heart and trust of their child. But, and this should be obvious, you can't "train a child in the way he should go" unless you know which way you want him to go!

Sympathy, encouragement, and nurture are important aspects of directive discipline. There is a big difference between leading a child who wants to follow you and having to push a child who resists your leading. If you want your child to follow your direction, you have to do the relational work that will turn your child's heart toward yours. But there is one remaining aspect to directive discipline, and it is the key to discipline in all of its expressions—instruction. Without instruction, there is no real biblical discipline.

Every major passage that deals directly with bringing up children touches on instruction. God has delegated to parents alone the responsibility to instruct their children in His ways. However, it's also clear that instruction and learning about faith are to take place within a community of faith where God's truth is lived out. As we see in both the Old and New Testaments, the community of faith also provides instruction to children through certain rituals, gatherings, feasts, readings, holidays, temple events, assemblies (church), fellowship, preaching, modeling, and more. However, the instruction gained from the community of faith affirms and reinforces, but never usurps, the discipline and instruction that is to be received at home. The following two key passages underscore parental instruction, one from the Old Testament and one from the New Testament:

> These words, which I am commanding you today, shall be on your heart. *You shall teach them diligently to your sons* and shall *talk of them* when you sit in your house and when you walk by the way and when you lie down and when you rise up. You shall *bind them* as a sign on your hand and they shall be as frontals on your forehead. You shall *write them* on the doorposts of your house and on your gates. (Deuteronomy 6:6-9; see also 11:18-19)

Children, obey your parents in the Lord, for this is right. Honor your father and mother (which is the first commandment with a promise), so that it may be well with you, and that you may live long on the earth. Fathers, do not provoke your children to anger, but *bring them up in the discipline and instruction of the Lord.* (Ephesians 6:1-4)[1]

In the Deuteronomy passage, "teaching [God's truth] diligently" refers not to impersonal instructional procedure, but to the natural overflow of truth that is already in the parents' hearts. If it is not there, it's because the parents have not heeded the command to put it there.

When he repeated the command later, Moses made the point even stronger: "You shall therefore impress these words of mine *on your heart* and *on your soul*" (Deuteronomy 11:18). The classroom for this kind of overflowing instruction is the life of the family. Instruction should be happening everywhere—"when you sit in your house and when you walk by the way"; and all the time—"when you lie down and when you rise up" (Deuteronomy 6:7). Even the physical house where the family lives should give evidence of God's truth, just as the Israelites wrote God's Word on their doorposts and gates.

In the Ephesians passage, Paul first reminded children to give heed to the instruction that is expected from their parents ("obey your parents") and to God's command ("Honor your father and mother" [see Exodus 20:12]). Then Paul commanded fathers to bring up their children in the "discipline and instruction of the Lord." The term for "discipline" (*paidea*, NIV "training") suggests corrective instruction that leads a child into living righteously. "Instruction" *(nouthesia)* comes from two words that literally mean "to place in the mind." It is often translated "admonish" (as in giving a warning), but it implies personal warmth and closeness. Paul told the Colossians, "We proclaim Him, *admonishing* every man and teaching every man with all wisdom, so that we may present every man complete in

Christ" (1:28). For parents, "every man" is their children, and only instruction that is "of the Lord" will result in a child who grows up to be "complete in Christ."

When the Bible speaks about instruction, it is speaking about more than just the transmission of information about God. Many parents have slipped into believing that increasing their children's knowledge about God and the Bible—memory verses, Bible books, catechisms, Bible stories—fulfills the biblical requirement that parents instruct their children in God's truth. While all of those tools may be helpful and beneficial, using them doesn't equate to biblical parental instruction, especially if it's done by others in Sunday school and Bible club or impersonally through books and tapes. Children need their parents' personal instruction.

Dr. Lawrence Richards, an authority and prolific author in the fields of Christian education and Bible teaching, makes the following point: "It is not enough to gain mental mastery of biblical information. The divine word must be taken into the very heart of the learner and expressed in his every choice and act.… Just as in the Old Testament era, the teaching that Scripture finds significant is not that which provides information alone but also the teaching that creates disciples who live in responsive obedience to God's will."[2] Unfortunately, too many Christian parents are settling for information rather than transformation.

INSTRUCTION VERSUS INFORMATION

In the Bible, the idea of instruction or teaching is like a transparent thread running from cover to cover. It's there, tying all the truths of Scripture together, but we tend to look right through it. All of Scripture is a revelation, or a revealing of truth, by the Creator God to His creatures. We know about God because of what He has revealed to us through His chosen messengers, but most of all through His Son. He wants us to know how we can restore our relationship with Him (that's the gospel), what His plan for His creation is, and how we can live in a way that will please Him and bring the greatest blessings (and eternal rewards) to us. The singular role of instruction is to make that mulitfaceted message known. But knowledge of God alone is never the goal of instruction. The goal is a transformed life that reflects God's reality and His truth.

As Jesus ascended to heaven, He left us with these words: "Go therefore and *make disciples* of all the nations, baptizing them in the name of the Father and the Son and the Holy Spirit, *teaching them to observe all that I commanded you...*" (Matthew 28:19-20). The term "make disciples" literally means "make learners," so Jesus' disciples were to go out "teaching" everyone to follow the pattern of life He had first taught them. Every parent who follows Christ has a twofold command: First, parents are to "baptize" their children when they become followers of Christ. This instruction probably has more in view than just a dip in the water. Baptism is the means by which a new follower of Christ publicly identifies with and becomes accountable to the community of faith. Second, parents are to "teach" their children what Christ taught, as well as all the scriptures that teach *about* Christ.

Jesus was a rabbi who followed the same pattern as other Jewish rabbis. His disciples (learners) lived and traveled with Him, absorbing His teaching and wisdom with one goal in view—to become like Him. That's why Jesus said, "A pupil [literally, a disciple or learner] is not above his teacher; but everyone, after he has been fully trained, will be like his teacher" (Luke 6:40). Biblical instruction is not just about knowing what the teacher knows, but about becoming *like* the teacher ("to observe all that I commanded you"). It's about life transformation. That's why Paul, the greatest teacher of Christianity after Jesus Himself, not only instructed but admonished others to follow his example of following Christ. He commanded believers, "Do not be conformed to this world, but be transformed by the renewing of your mind" (Romans 12:2). This is what Scripture directs me to do with my children. I am both the model and the missionary of the transformed life. Through my directive discipline in their lives, they will follow my guidance.

Like many areas related to communication, though, parents have seen their role as instructors challenged by a growing number of outside influences. Radio, television, magazines, the Internet, and other media consume more and more of the hours that people once spent together as a family. Between the Civil War and World War I, many hours of the week that are now consumed by media were spent together with family members, relaxing, talking, and reading aloud. The printed word reigned supreme, so it was common practice in Victorian Christian homes to have daily Scripture readings or a weekly "home circle." This time was reserved for parental, usually fatherly, instruction in the Scriptures.

The breakup of the home circle has had a far-reaching impact, but we take this situation pretty much for granted because the change came gradually. We have lost a great deal with the advent of media in the post-Victorian era, and that fact is obvious in several areas. First, media has become a primary source of instruction, for good or bad, usurping that role from parents. Children now acquire most of their information about the world from various media sources. Second, children have become conditioned by media to expect instruction to happen in segments of minutes, for it to be highly visual, and for it to come predigested in discrete bits and pieces. This fragmentation of information both trivializes truth and hinders a child's ability to think critically. Third, mass media has resulted in a lower quality of content in order to speak to a mass audience. Though there are some rich examples of quality content, the media ocean is culture-wide and very, very shallow. Finally, basic parental knowledge and the skills necessary to instruct children have essentially been lost due to lack of use. Without those interpersonal communication skills, parents are limited to filling their children's brains with more bits of truth, unable to reach their hearts with transforming truth.

We can't turn back the clock to return to a "simpler" time, but neither should we simply admit defeat in the battle for more of our children's time. Complacency in our responsibility to instruct our children allows other "instructors" to take our place. We need to reclaim our roles as instructors.

PUTTING A FACE ON INSTRUCTION

Instruction, as an element of directive discipline, is an act of love on par with sympathy, encouragement, and nurture. Solomon wrote, "My son, do not reject the discipline of the LORD or loathe His reproof, for whom the LORD loves He reproves, even as a father corrects the son in whom he delights" (Proverbs 3:11-12).

Here's the question, though: What needs to be reclaimed in order for parents to become effective at instruction? Scripture suggests two main aspects of instruction apart from the actual content: function and form. Function is what instruction is meant to accomplish. Paul describes some of those functions in 2 Timothy 3:16, saying that Scripture is profitable for "teaching" (imparting truth), "reproof" (pointing out sin), "correction" (guiding away from sin), and "training in righteousness" (guiding into God's ways). On the surface, I would say that most Christian parents feel comfortable with the more functional parts of instruction—they can apply a scripture to a child's life and get the information across.

But what about the form of instruction? Parents have lost not so much the content and function of Scripture, but rather the skill of communicating truth effectively. Parents can still communicate knowledge (information) to their children's *minds,* but we have lost the skills that enable us to better reach our children's *hearts.* The sea of information-based resources and products is almost endless—books, workbooks, videos, tapes, DVDs, Web sites, and so on. But such tools quickly become a kind of hit-and-run instruction that relies more on the impersonal product for instruction than on the personal relationship. Remember, information without transformation is not biblical instruction, and transformation comes only through relationship.

So as we consider the form of instruction, we need to consider the way that truth and information are communicated. If content is about *what* is said, and function is *why* something is said, then form is *how* something is said. Paul probably wanted to emphasize the *how* of the instruction he and Silas provided for the Thessalonians when he described their words as "exhorting and encouraging and imploring each one of you as a father would his own children" (1 Thessalonians 2:11). He was picturing a father instructing his children with passion and urgency. The father in this verse is certainly doing more than just passing along information—he is putting biblical truth into a form that emphasizes its importance.

But form also can be a method of instruction. Jesus was a masterful communicator who employed a variety of methods, including parables. He could have simply stated a bare truth, such as "God is a faithful Father who welcomes back repentant sons." Rather than simply inform, though, Jesus showed the truth by telling the parable of the prodigal son. He also used metaphors and illustrations, such as comparing faith to a mustard seed. He told stories using familiar images, like a house built on sand. And he often used questions to make a point, such as when he asked what father would give his child a stone instead of bread, or a snake instead of fish. Jesus turned everyday items into object lessons, associating deep spiritual truths with little sparrows and lilies in the field. When you read the accounts of Jesus' interactions with His followers, you can imagine Him looking into a listener's eyes, speaking directly, and touching a shoulder. When preaching was needed, He would speak confidently and loudly enough to be heard by hundreds. When counsel was needed, He would speak softly and personally. Sometimes He would not speak at all, but make mud out of spittle and dirt and use it to heal a blind person or simply write on the ground with a finger.

If you are serious about instructing your child in a way that will not just inform but transform, then pattern your instruction after Jesus' example. Imitating Jesus' instructional form is part of the process of being "fully trained" to be like your teacher (see Luke 6:40). Let's recapture the form of effective instruction by practicing the practical and proven methods of instruction seen in Scripture. As you consider these instructional forms and methods, ask the Lord, by the power of the Spirit, to enable you to grow in your instructional skills.

Storytelling

Jesus told stories—interesting, captivating, convicting, memorable stories. He communicated profound and life-changing truth through simple stories featuring the prodigal son, ten lepers, a dishonest steward, a good Samaritan, and many others. Jesus demonstrated how truth can be powerfully transmitted when harnessed to a story. In the same way that saying, "Don't think about a blue horse," assures that you will, the well-told story will be remembered because of the vivid mental images it evokes.

Children respond to stories for the simple reason that they can visualize truth even though they may not understand the truth completely. A picture may not be worth quite a thousand words to a child with limited vocabulary, but there is no doubting a story's instructional value. So why don't we tell more stories to our children? Probably because we've delegated that role to the visual media and because it takes time—a scarce resource that is getting scarcer—to tell stories.

Sally and I have used storytelling in numerous ways. Retelling Bible stories or parables using updated, age-related settings and language is an obvious use of storytelling. As we retell the stories of Gideon or Elijah, the instruction or lesson comes with the story, and we might add other scripture. When our children were younger, we used made-up stories to apply a biblical principle to a specific situation, such as a story about a brave young boy who overcomes great difficulty, to help that child have faith in Jesus to battle a nighttime fear. A scripture always accompanies the story, of course. For older children, a biblical truth might be illuminated by a real-life story from our own past, or from the family, or from history. Particularly effective in corrective discipline are stories I share from my own childhood, or even my adult life, about committing a certain sin and then being corrected. A parent's personal story softens and opens a child's heart like little else can.

Besides being an effective means of communication, storytelling is essential to directive discipline. But using this tool well takes practice. If you have not used storytelling before, start small. Try retelling a Bible story in your own words, or practice the skill by telling some personal or family stories at the dinner table. Then, pray for the Holy Spirit to alert you to opportunities to use storytelling to instruct your children. Stories are especially useful when decisions need to be made, bad attitudes flare, conflicts arise with friends, and for various bedtime issues. Many instructional opportunities do not call for a story, of course, but be ready for the ones that do. The most important thing to remember is that a good story can't be rushed. If you can reclaim some of the time that you typically lose to the mass media, you'll have more time for using the power of storytelling in your family. And more time with your family will give you more inroads into your children's hearts.

Illustration

Preachers use illustrations for good reason: Thoughtful, well-timed illustrations illuminate biblical truth. You can remember a number of sermon illustrations and their meaning even though you can't recall the content of the sermon itself. Your children are no different.

Sally has a real talent for using illustrations. An example is a question our children used to ask about why our family spent so much time talking about Scripture and the Christian life. To answer their question, Sally asked the children to imagine that we had a big treasure chest for each of them, and every day they would see us putting something into each chest. The chests would be theirs to keep when they grew up. If they opened the chests and found mostly rocks, they would feel cheated. But if they found gold and jewels, they would feel grateful. That illustration explained why Sally and I put scripture into their hearts every day. We were (and still are) storing up treasure for heaven, and when they are grown they will be thankful that their hearts are full of what we've put there (see Matthew 6:20-21).

God's truth is still powerful apart from the use of illustrations and stories, but when you are instructing your child about a Bible passage or truth and you're just not connecting, a simple illustration of the truth can make it come alive. Ask the Spirit of God to help you fill in the blank, "Well, it's like ———."

Questions

Questions are typical table talk in our home. "So, Joel, how do you think God would've wanted you to respond when that boy got so angry with you?" A good discussion then ensues, involving principles such as "a gentle answer turns away wrath" (Proverbs 15:1) and Jesus' command to turn the other cheek (see Luke 6:29). We could also talk about patience and self-control as the fruit of the Holy Spirit (see Galatians 5:22-23) and the example of Christ: "While being reviled, He did not revile in return" and "while suffering, He uttered no threats, but kept entrusting Himself to Him who judges righteously" (1 Peter 2:23). And all of this can grow out of one simple question.

But clearly, there is an art to asking good questions. Whether you're trying to draw out a response, test a child's understanding, or stimulate a good discussion, the discussion that follows greatly depends on the quality of your question. A poor question will elicit only awkward silence, uncertain responses, or hopeful "Is that the right answer Daddy?" looks. When interacting with your children, a question should be more invitation than investigation or interrogation. If invited properly, your children will gladly respond to your question.[3]

What is true about asking questions that lead to learning is also true about the power of questions for directive discipline. As you are directing your child along the path of life, a timely and good question has the ability both to help you connect with your child's heart and to get a closer look at how well your child is understanding and internalizing biblical truths and principles. But what makes a good question? In my experience, it's a question that is simple, short, strategic, and stimulating. There are also certain types of questions to avoid:

- *Close-ended questions* that can be answered only with a yes or no, I don't know, or by one of your either-or choices
- *Loaded questions* that include your hidden agenda, such as your desire to admonish or correct your child
- *Rhetorical questions* that raise issues a child can't answer
- *Values clarification questions* that are morally or ethically vague or promote moral relativism

Persuasion

If you grew up in a church from the revivalist tradition, red flags may pop up when you hear the word *persuasion.* The dark side of religious persuasion is emotional manipulation—making one feel guilty, browbeating a person into a decision or action, or talking a person into making a choice. Certainly there is a human-centered kind of persuasion, but there is also a legitimate biblical persuasion that comes from a heartfelt conviction. Paul said to the Corinthians, "Therefore, knowing the fear of the Lord, we persuade men..." (2 Corinthians 5:11). Even more to the point, when he spoke of his instruction to the Thessalonians, he described it as "imploring each one of you as a father would his own children" (1 Thessalonians 2:11).

Throughout the Bible, and especially when it comes to the gospel in the New Testament, truth is communicated with a sense of spiritual and emotional urgency. It's an appeal to the heart and the conscience that goes further than simply communicating information. It's a passionate appeal to come around to God's way of thinking. Read the book of Acts, especially the first twelve chapters, to taste the passion and emotion of the preaching and teaching that stirred the hearts of the early believers. This preaching often included warning, but it was even more focused on and motivated by hope and desire.

If your children never sense passion and urgency in your instruction, then you are silently teaching them that biblical truth is nothing more than information they need to know or rules that they need to keep. If you want your children to desire to have the life of Christ that is within you, then your instruction must reveal your genuine excitement about God's truth.

In calling persuasion a method of instruction, I don't want to suggest that you should force yourself to be passionate. If you are a controlled person emotionally, ask the Holy Spirit to give you greater freedom of expression. If the joy of the Lord isn't evident in your instruction, then you're not walking in the power of the Holy Spirit, and your discipline and instruction will be fruitless. If you want to reach your children's hearts with your instruction, then your instruction needs to come from more than just your mind. Your children need to hear, and feel, what God's truth really means to your heart. That is heartfelt discipline.

Object Lessons

Jesus taught a brief but powerful object lesson when He pointed into the sky and said, "Look at the birds of the air, that they do not sow, nor reap nor gather into barns, and yet your heavenly Father feeds them. Are you not worth much more than they?" (Matthew 6:26). He used a real object to teach a lesson: Birds don't worry, and neither should you.

You'll see object lessons everywhere if you train yourself to look for them. A candle in a dark room becomes a lesson about being light in our dark world. A squirrel putting away nuts for the winter becomes a lesson about diligence. Feathers dropped in front of a spinning fan blade become a lesson about the rapid spread of gossip. There are volumes of books describing useful object lessons, but the best lessons are those that come from you and are tailor-made to your child's current needs. It's a method of instruction that, especially with younger children, creates a bridge to truth. When teachable moments come along, it's good to use a physical object to make a spiritual point, just as Jesus did.

Narration

Narration is a venerable but often unnamed method of instruction that can be useful for directive discipline. Narration involves telling back or writing down, in your child's words, what has been heard or read. It's a modern-day equivalent of passing down truth by oral tradition in which learners would repeat the lessons of their teachers until those ideas had become a part of their own thinking. A Jewish rabbi didn't have printed Torah study guides to hand out to his students—he expected them to listen attentively to his lessons, and he drove his points deep into their minds through repetition and memorization. Narration is a simple form of instruction that will help you do the same thing with your children.

Here's how it works. You train your children to know that whenever the Bible is read in your home, they will be expected to listen carefully and be ready to repeat back what they have heard. If you read the story of Joseph being sold into slavery, your children should be able at any point to "narrate" what they've heard. Even if you're reading Romans, you can still expect your child to attempt a narration. You'll need to start with small portions of Scripture and work up to longer ones, but as your children are trained in the art of narration, their powers of attention and retention will grow, as will their ability to synthesize and communicate ideas and concepts. This process also causes them to internalize what they hear and to grow in their powers of reasoning and self-expression. The method of teaching narration is quite easy: The next time you read to your children from Scripture, ask them to tell you in their own words what you have just read. Writing down what they have heard is also a form of narration.

INSTRUCTION ON THE PATH OF LIFE

According to the Bible, there is no discipline without instruction, and biblical instruction involves transformation, not just information. Paul reminded Timothy that the goal of his instruction was "love from a pure heart and a good conscience and a sincere faith" (1 Timothy 1:5). Paul's goal was a transformed life. It's easy to pour Bible facts and information into your child's brain, but if your instruction isn't heartfelt, it will merely inform without transforming. Biblical instruction—biblical discipline—must come from the overflow of your own heart and connect with your child's heart to produce fruit. As you lead your children along the path of life, they need regular, daily exposure to your loving, heartfelt instruction.

✛

PART III

CORRECTIVE

DISCIPLINE

SPIRITUAL DISCIPLINE

Parenting Through the Power of Grace

When it comes to the rubber-meets-the-road issue of corrective discipline, there is no shortage of advice on what to do, how to do it, and when to do it. Biblical discipline, however, involves much more than merely correcting your children. Discipline is the entire process by which we lead another person toward a righteous life.

Biblical discipline, what we're calling heartfelt discipline, begins with directive discipline, by which we direct a child along the path of life. This is the necessary starting point because children can't know they are doing wrong if they don't first know how to do right. However, for most Christian parents, corrective discipline makes up the lion's share of their disciplinary efforts. And when they think of taking corrective measures, they often picture some very hands-on approaches. There is much in Scripture that is left out of that equation.

In the many books on childhood discipline that I have read, I've noticed a common characteristic—the books focus on what the *parent* should do. To a large degree, that makes sense for a how-to book. But few, if any, of these books open our eyes to *God's* role in childhood discipline. If childhood discipline is, at its heart, a spiritual issue, and if God is involved in it, shouldn't He be every parent's starting point? If my first impulse is to determine the best how-to method of discipline while basically ignoring the spiritual side, can I expect to achieve the right result? Do

I relegate God to the role of divine bystander in the discipline process, or is He an active participant? And if He is intimately involved, then am I intimately involved with Him?

These questions go back to the issue of parental control: Am I in control when I discipline, or is the Holy Spirit in charge? But let's shift the focus and make this a question of effectiveness: Does my child respond to my discipline because of my superlative techniques, because of God's presence, or because of both? From my reading, I've seen that the experts most often encourage parents to put their confidence in a method rather than in God. Now I can understand some parents who feel that spiritual discipline doesn't sound measurable or truly effective. Can it really be trusted, these parents might ask, to solve a serious problem they're having with their child *right now?* The answer is yes. Spiritual discipline, if properly understood, is the most effective priority of childhood discipline. It's the heart and soul of corrective discipline.

LAW VERSUS GRACE

I'm not some weird mystic, and I'm not even a superspiritual person. In my unredeemed heart I'm a Pharisee. I'd be a great rule maker and rule enforcer, and I really do look good in a black robe. However, in my grace-touched heart, I want to be more like Jesus—acknowledging the rules but looking to the heart. Rather than seeing my value in how well I perform, I want to see my value in how well I love God and people (in this discussion, my kids). My life is a constant struggle between those two desires, and so is yours. It's the battle between law and grace that we see described in Scripture.

Parents see this battle regularly played out on the field of childhood discipline. I know for certain that it's quicker and easier just to lay down the law than it is to offer grace. Plus, somewhere in my mind the argument gets made that my child is an unredeemed sinner and therefore is in need of law to restrain that sin. That's true to a degree, but if I stop there, then law prevails over grace. My child needs grace to learn how to choose not to sin and instead choose to obey God.

A parenting model based on law tends to result in discipline characterized by regulations. It focuses more on what children are doing wrong than on what they could be doing right. In that approach, the motivation to do right is to avoid punishment for doing wrong. On the other hand, a parenting model based on grace will tend to result in relationship-based discipline. The grace model doesn't overlook wrongdoing, but it adds the wisdom and insight of a parent who can see what children are becoming and what they could become in the future.

Both approaches—grace and law—recognize the reality of sin in a child's life and the need to deal with it. However, it's a whole lot easier to discipline by law. The approach of grace and relationship takes a lot of time. That's why the less time we spend with our children, the more we tend to rely on law. Regulations replace relationship, and a quick guilt trip takes the place of any expression of understanding and love. But the biblical reality is that we grow through grace, not through the law. Law shows us our need for a Savior, but it can't change us because it's all about externals. Grace alone changes us from the inside out to help us become like the Savior. My children need some law, but even more they need grace.

Grace is an active expression of God's love toward us. Paul even personified grace to some degree when he wrote to Titus, describing grace as a gift bearer (even the word for grace, *charis,* means "a favor bestowed"). Paul finished giving instructions about how elders, older men, older women, young women, young men, and slaves are to conduct themselves as Christians. Actually, it sounds a lot like regulations. But then, in the next sentence, he explained *why* they should follow these rules: "For the grace of God has appeared, bringing salvation to all men" (Titus 2:11). The reason we should live by God's ways is because God, out of His limitless love and mercy and goodness, has saved us. We were lost, but now we are saved—only because of His grace.

Then Paul reminded Titus exactly what grace does. First, it has come "instructing us to deny ungodliness and worldly desires" (Titus 2:12). It teaches us to say no to whatever is not of God. That sounds a lot like a parent, doesn't it? Interestingly, the Greek word for "instructing" is *paideuo,* which is the same word used to refer to the discipline of a young child, and comes from the same word family as the word *discipline* in Ephesians 6:4. Grace is the internal parent that disciplines the spirit to choose to say no when tempted by sin and worldly desires.

But that's not all grace does. Second, grace has come "instructing us… to live sensibly, righteously and godly in the present age" (Titus 2:12). That same internal parent also disciplines the spirit to say yes to the things of God. Grace helps us choose sensible and godly words and behaviors and to walk on the way of righteousness.

Paul left no doubt as to the motivation for our behavior. We follow God because His grace has us "looking for the blessed hope and the appearing of the glory of our great God and Savior, Christ Jesus, who gave Himself for us to redeem us from every lawless deed, and to purify for Himself a people for His own possession, zealous for good deeds" (Titus 2:13-14). We follow God because of relationship—God's love for us and His desire to have us for Himself.

Grace is God's work in our hearts that enables us to know Him. Any attempt to reach God by doing "good" things to try to earn His favor is fruitless. There is no way around our sin except through God's grace. He has not only saved us, but He helps us live as saved people. His grace enables us to please Him.

PARENTING THROUGH GRACE

When your child is arguing with you rather than simply obeying your request, how does grace help you? Without the grace of God Paul spoke of, your discipline is limited to external controls. Only grace enables you to reach your child's heart, the spiritual dimension where the Holy Spirit can work. That is the target of spiritual discipline. When you correct your child, you want to know that you are working on both the external behavior and the internal understanding. But only God's grace allows you to reach inside.

God has created channels through which His grace can come into our lives. We call these the "means of grace," and in the evangelical tradition there are three: God's Word, prayer, and fellowship. You open a channel for God's grace to flow into your life when He speaks to you (through His Word), when you speak to Him (through prayer), and when He speaks to and through you with other Christians (through fellowship).

Your children experience God's grace to the degree that you open the channels into your own life and become a channel of grace for them. God has designed childhood to be a time of openness to Him and His work. In the same way that your children depend on you for food to grow physically, they also depend on you to be a channel of God's grace that enables them to grow spiritually. They can begin to open those channels for themselves, but if you aren't receiving grace into your life by reading God's Word, praying, and having meaningful fellowship with other believers, then you are hindering the grace your children are meant to experience through you. You must be receiving grace in order to give it. Your own relationship to God is the key to your children's relationship to God, which is the key to your effectiveness in corrective discipline.

If you ignore spiritual discipline and go straight to the practical aspects of corrective discipline (verbal, behavioral, and physical), then you're in danger of relying on law, which can control behavior but can't help your children grow spiritually. Growth in righteousness is the goal of all biblical discipline, so be sure your children are receiving everything they need to grow. You can be assured that this is happening when you give attention to the means of grace in your own life.

Open the Channel of God's Word

Your children need to see that you believe the Bible is more than just a religious rule book. Of course, they need instruction in the Word, and of course they need to know what is right and wrong, but they also need to see that the Word of God is "living and active," in the sense that it adds a spiritual reality to your life (see Hebrews 4:12). Jesus condemned the Pharisees for twisting the Old Testament Law into spirit-killing rules: The Pharisees applied Scripture in a way that killed the spirit rather than giving it life. Paul said, speaking of the Law, that "the letter kills, but the Spirit gives life" (2 Corinthians 3:6). Spiritual discipline brings the life of the Spirit into your corrective discipline.

Seeking Guidance

In our home, Sally and I talk about what God's Word says to our children about how they live their lives, about sins to avoid, about attitudes, about loving others, about being like Christ. Those are all necessary for correcting our children (and we'll look at verbal correction in the next chapter). But we also talk about what we, Mom and Dad, are learning from Scripture. We share insights that God has brought to our hearts about self-control, about being patient and long-suffering, about seeing the good in our children, about being under the control of the Holy Spirit in our discipline, about loving our kids without expectations, about offering them grace.

We want our children to know that their parents are hearing from God on a regular basis and that what God is saying affects how we relate to them. God's Word is more than just tips and truths; it is literally a "word from God." Through the Word and prayer, Sally and I are carrying on a daily conversation with the God of the universe who has things He wants us to learn. Our children see that we are listening to God because He is disciplining us, through His Word, to help us grow in the same way we are disciplining them. If God's Word is "living and active" in our lives, then it can be in the lives of our children as well.

Claiming Promises

It's one thing for our children to see that we are listening to God, but it's another for them to see that we believe His promises. Of course, it's easy to believe the big promises of what will happen in the future and about salvation and heaven, but what about the promises of wisdom for today (see James 1:5), or that God will provide for our financial needs (see Philippians 4:19), or that God will right a wrong (see Romans 12:17-19)? When children see parents believing God, in faith, for things He promises in His Word, the Scriptures come alive.

For corrective discipline, though, it is especially grace-giving to pray a promise or claim a verse specifically for your child. When a child is corrected for messing up, her parents bring grace when they apply a verse to her life: "For I am confident of this very thing, that He who began a good work in you, [name of your child], will perfect it until the day of Christ Jesus" (Philippians 1:6).

Praying Scripture

The idea behind praying Scripture is simple: Let the words *of* God be your words *to* God. In a sense, you let Him put words in your mouth. You can pray some scriptures directly to God, others you might quote and then apply to a situation in your family, and still others you can paraphrase and pray back to Him. The idea, though, is to allow Scripture itself to become a part of your prayers for your children. Then you're not just praying Mom or Dad's words; you're praying God's words.[1]

Open the Channel of Prayer

It should be evident that prayer is indispensable to spiritual discipline. When you correct your child without the presence of God, your action will be nothing more than an act of parental discipline. But when you stop and pray about the matter, the focus shifts from your authority to God's. A silent prayer helps only you, but a spoken prayer helps orient your child to the spiritual nature of the discipline. When you place the matter before God, even if your child doesn't fully understand the correction, he still becomes accountable to God. Your spoken prayer reminds your child that "there is no creature [or child] hidden from His sight, but all things are open and laid bare to the eyes of Him with whom we have to do" (Hebrews 4:13).

Prayer opens the channel of grace from this side of the earthly-heavenly divide. It is an act of faith that affirms that Mom and Dad believe that there is a God, that He is personal, that He loves us, and that He cares about the choices we make. The grace brought into your children's lives by your example of prayer will have a powerful influence on how they will relate to God. As that grace helps them grow, it will turn their spirits toward God. The act of praying as part of the process of corrective discipline is therefore a powerful key to bringing life to your child's spirit.

Praying for Your Child's Spirit

Corrective discipline will help your child learn to say no to what is wrong and yes to what is right. Christian parents want to see that happen as a result of a child's changed spirit. We want our children to desire in their hearts to please us because they understand to some degree that obeying their parents pleases God. We long to see our children's will directed by a spirit that is responding to God.

To see these desires fulfilled, we must pray for them. If we really believe that corrective discipline is more than just behavior control, and if we really believe that discipline is a spiritual process that keeps our children on God's path of life, shouldn't we also believe that the most important thing we can do for our children is to pray for God to work in their hearts? The degree to which we fail to pray for our children is the degree to which we would rather rely on our own methods and techniques.

So commit yourself to pray for your children. Pray for responsive spirits, soft hearts, and willing minds. Pray that God will remind them of scriptures, that they will feel convicted when they sin, and that, on their own, they will say no to sin. Pray that God will let you catch them doing wrong so you can correct them, that He will let you catch them doing right so you can encourage them, and that He will protect them from evil. Pray for godly friends who will spur them on to good deeds, for growing insight about living for God, and for discipline in beginning to read the Bible to find direction. And here's the important part: Tell your children what you have prayed for them in private, and also make a point to pray these things with them or in their hearing.

Praying with Your Child

My wife, Sally, is a pray-about-it-now person who interjects lots of prayers into our family life. I'm not talking about prayer at meals, but morning devotions, during-the-day petitions for whatever comes up, times of praise and thanksgiving, opportunities when families come over, and, of course, at bedtime. Sally pours grace into our children's lives many times each day by stopping to pray with them. Her ears are open to issues that can be brought before God, so she is always initiating prayers with and for our children as well as responding to requests from them.

When corrective discipline is called for, it's even more important to take the initiative and pray with your child about the matter at hand. The child needs to be prayed for, but also to pray. When you pray for your child to be convicted of a sin and to respond to God's correction, you set the stage for him to confess that sin and to pray for forgiveness and new resolve to resist it. Prayer makes the sin not just a mistake but a serious matter of the spirit.

Open the Channel of Fellowship

When children sin, their natural response is to hide the sin and to separate themselves emotionally and spiritually from you. Adam and Eve hid themselves from God because they didn't want to face Him after disobeying, and that same dynamic is still at work. But God intends for us to "bear one another's burdens" (Galatians 6:2), to "spur one another on toward love and good deeds" (Hebrews 10:24, NIV), and to help one another since we are all in the same sinful boat. That's why we need fellowship with other believers. We are designed to be in fellowship with others because we are designed to find fellowship with God. Earthly fellowship reflects heavenly fellowship.

Your children need fellowship no less than you do. They need to see that all people sin and feel guilty, that God forgives them, and that others still love them. Fellowship keeps your children from withdrawing into themselves when they sin. It also keeps them accountable to other believers. As a means of grace, the love and forgiveness of others makes real and tangible the love and forgiveness of God.

Relating One on One

Jesus declared that "where two or three have gathered together in My name, I am there in their midst" (Matthew 18:20). Christ is with those who seek His wisdom. You and your child are two, and when you are together you can assure your child that Christ is right there with you. When the issue is corrective discipline, be sure your child knows that Christ is there with you not as a Judge, but as a Helper. Assure your child that you are not separated from each other, but that even in discipline you can have fellowship with each other and with Christ who is with you.

On a more proactive course, though, be sure to make time to fellowship with your child one-on-one throughout the week. Get away together and just talk. Encourage your child in some areas of growth, tell her how you are praying for her, share a scripture with her. Such times will mean closer fellowship that will reduce the separation factor when there is sin that needs to be corrected. That fellowship with you will bring the grace of God into the lives of your children in a very real and tangible way.

Relating to Like-Minded Families

You probably wouldn't think about fellowship with other families as a factor in spiritual discipline, and especially not a part of corrective discipline, but it is an important piece of the puzzle. If you are to bring the grace of God into your children's lives, they need to see that other families love God just as your family does. They need to see other parents who discipline their children the way you do, who say the kinds of things you do, who trust and follow God the way you do. If your child suspects that your family is really "out there" spiritually, then your discipline will be lumped together with that false perception.

Even more, though, your children need Christian fellowship to affirm the spiritual realities you are trying to bring into your home life. Make time to fellowship with like-minded families not only for fun but also for Bible study, a time of sharing and prayer, or a sing-along. Start a class at church that is age-integrated so whole families are able to study the Bible and learn together. Plan an outreach ministry that families can do together. All these activities will bring the grace of God into your child's life as well as put your discipline into a bigger frame of reference.

SPIRITUAL DISCIPLINE ALONG THE PATH OF LIFE

When used skillfully and faithfully, the spiritual aspects of corrective discipline will affect how you use the other tools of verbal, behavioral, and physical discipline. When you see that your child needs corrective discipline, reach first for spiritual discipline. Pray for your child's spirit, ask God for applicable scriptures, seek to establish fellowship—and then do what you need to do to address the misbehavior or disobedient action. If you know you've done the work of spiritual discipline first, then you'll feel more confident that the rest of your discipline will reflect the Bible's requirements as well.

CHAPTER 10

VERBAL DISCIPLINE

Speaking Wise Words to Correct What's Wrong

Thirteen-year-old Jeremy got into a scrape in the neighborhood when another boy called him a name and then continued the verbal assault. Jeremy reached his limit and took steps to end the harangue. His dad, working in the yard, heard the commotion and broke the boys up before things got out of hand.

"Dad, I couldn't help myself," Jeremy explained when his father took him inside. "When he started arguing with me and egging me on, I kind of lost it. I told him to stop, and then I pushed him. That's all...really."

Jeremy was telling his dad the truth as he saw it, but he needed the perspective of a parent to open his eyes to the bigger picture. He needed to view his response to the other boy in light of biblical wisdom and God's commands regarding how we handle anger. In the book of Ephesians, God doesn't condemn *feeling* angry, but He warns against *expressing* anger in a sinful way (see 4:26). And Paul explained that anger has the potential to "give the devil an opportunity" to cause us to sin (Ephesians 4:27).

"Is that what happened today?" Jeremy's father asked, after they looked at the Ephesians passage.

"Man, God got that one right! But what should I have done?"

At this point, Jeremy was ready to hear how God's Word could help him the next time he was angry and tempted to exercise bad judgment.

James offers a useful solution: "Be quick to hear, slow to speak and slow to anger; for the anger of man does not achieve the righteousness of God" (1:19-20).

"Sometimes," Jeremy's dad told him, "you just have to slow down the anger you feel inside. It's like making a conscious decision to turn down the heat underneath a pot of water. Once that anger boils over, sin is in charge, and someone's going to get burned."

"That's exactly what it feels like when it happens," Jeremy agreed. "But how do I turn down that feeling of anger?"

His dad answered the question from Scripture. "Paul described two kinds of people in Galatians 5. He described those who are known by their deeds of the flesh—that is, their sins—which include 'outbursts of anger, disputes, [and] dissensions.' Then he described those who are known by the fruit of the Spirit, which is 'love, joy, peace, patience, kindness, goodness, faithfulness, gentleness, self-control' [see verses 16-26]. Which kind of person would you rather be known as?"

In his heart, Jeremy wanted to conform to the second description. "I feel really uncomfortable around guys who seem pushy and angry all the time," he said. "I guess the fruit of the Spirit is sort of like 'What Would Jesus Do?' kinds of things."

"That's right!" his dad said. "It's being like Jesus. But it doesn't just happen. If you want the fruit of the Spirit, you need to ask God to help you grow it in your heart. And you have to make choices that will keep it growing. That's what it means to become mature and to live in a way that God calls 'righteous'. Does that make sense to you?"

Jeremy was beginning to understand, but he still needed help translating biblical principles into concrete action.

"The more you practice what God says," his father told him, "the more you will see His Holy Spirit working in your life."

Jeremy's dad could see that his son had a sensitive conscience and that his heart was open to God. "Look," he said, "the next time you feel anger starting to bubble up, start quoting Proverbs 15:1, 'A gentle answer turns away wrath.' Then turn that scripture into a prayer and ask God to give you a gentle answer to give the other person and see what happens."

Jeremy agreed to give it a try, and the two of them prayed together. The teenager confessed his sin of anger, and his dad prayed for him. The next step was for Jeremy to call the other boy and confess the wrongness of resorting to shoving. None of this was easy, but Jeremy's heart's desire was to obey God's requirements, and with his dad's help and support, he was able to make things right.

THE EFFECTIVE USE OF WORDS

God makes His will known to us primarily through words, so it makes sense that biblical discipline relies heavily on loving correction that is communicated in words. A parent's verbal instruction is meant to turn a child away from sin and toward righteousness. If a hidden camera followed some Christian parents around all day, however, a viewer might be tempted to conclude that verbal discipline means yelling, pleading, cajoling, and shaming a child into submission and obedience, but that's not a biblical picture. Correction doesn't stop with telling children what they've done wrong and what not to do in the future. Corrective discipline involves speaking the Word of God into a child's heart. God's truth, communicated in words, provides the corrective discipline, not a parent's high-volume rebuke.

In the scene that opened this chapter, the father could just as easily have criticized Jeremy for losing his temper, reminding him of family rules that prohibit physical responses such as shoving. "How many times have I warned you about your temper and the bad things it can lead to? I'm really disappointed in you." God's Word goes much further in correcting wrongs than do the scolding words of a parent.

Paul told Timothy that the Word of God is useful and beneficial to everyone who listens to it, no matter what their age (see 2 Timothy 3:16-

17). In four words Paul described what God's Word does—teach, reprove, correct, and train. Teaching sets the standard of godly living; reproof calls a person to account for violating God's ways; correction points the person in the right direction; and training (discipline) in righteousness directs the person toward godly living.

Each of these four words has a role in verbal discipline, but for now we'll concentrate on the middle two, which apply to the area of corrective discipline. The ministry of reproof involves using God's Word to point out error or sin in a person's life. The same Greek word is translated other places in the New Testament as "to expose," "to convict," and "to rebuke." Just three verses after using the term to describe what God's Word does, for instance, Paul used the same word in 2 Timothy 4:2 to charge Timothy to "*reprove,* rebuke, exhort, with great patience and instruction" those who won't listen to sound doctrine. The Word of God reproves both those who listen (like Timothy) and those who refuse to listen.

The ministry of correction uses God's Word to turn a child back toward the path of life. The Greek word is *epanorthosis,* from which we derive the English word *orthopedic.* The idea is to make something that has become crooked straight again, as an orthopedic surgeon would straighten a crooked limb. In terms of discipline, correction is the act of straightening out a child's behavior.

One commentator's summary brings the idea of correction home in a way that fits perfectly with the practice of heartfelt discipline: "In practice…the Scripture's own word of truth is the correcting agency. The believer who responds to God's word of correction will find himself lifted up and set on his feet, ready to travel along faith's pathway toward righteousness."[1] What a great picture of childhood discipline! You are correcting your children when they stumble or wander off in the wrong direction in order to set them walking again on the path of life.

The book of Proverbs speaks eloquently about reproof and rebuke. Consider just a few of the direct teachings about reproof:

My son, do not reject the discipline of the LORD
Or loathe His *reproof,*
For whom the LORD loves He *reproves,*
Even as a father corrects the son in whom he delights. (3:11-12)

He is on the path of life who heeds instruction,
But he who ignores *reproof* goes astray. (10:17)

A wise son accepts his father's discipline,
But a scoffer does not listen to *rebuke.* (13:1)

Poverty and shame will come to him who neglects discipline
    [instruction],
But he who regards *reproof* will be honored. (13:18)

He whose ear listens to the life-giving *reproof*
Will dwell among the wise. He who neglects discipline despises
    himself,
But he who listens to *reproof* acquires understanding. (15:31-32)

The wisdom of Proverbs makes it clear that there is no discipline without reproof. Correction is a necessary part of discipline, and the correction that counts most is that which comes from the Word of God. The Bible affirms throughout its pages that corrective discipline is typically delivered verbally.

DISCIPLINE THAT WORKS ON THE MIND

Your children can't obey what they don't know. For that reason, directive discipline (chapters 5–8) comes first.[2] You must lay the foundation of obedience by creating a loving relationship through sympathy, encouragement, nurture, and instruction. Corrective discipline (chapters 9–12) builds on that foundation, first spiritually by bringing God's grace into your discipline, and then verbally by bringing God's Word into it.

Verbal discipline is most effective for teaching your child what is right and what is wrong and how he can do what is right and avoid what is wrong. If your child has sinned, he needs to hear about it from you. It's the same principle that Paul described: "Faith comes from hearing, and hearing by the word of Christ" (Romans 10:17). The teachings of Christianity are preached and taught and passed on and explained—all through words. Your child needs to hear the correction of the Word of God coming from your mouth.

In a way, parents are cooperating with the ministry of the Holy Spirit in their child's heart and mind. Parents are conduits of God's grace at a time when their child may not have come into a full understanding of her need for Christ. Paul said in Romans 8:6 that "the mind set on the flesh is death, but the mind set on the Spirit is life and peace." When parents let the Word of God be the words of correction, they are helping their child set her mind on the Spirit. Parents are mediators of sorts who help their child know God's grace. It's all part of the process of preparing the soil of a child's heart for the gospel.

Biblical correction is always a matter of the Word of God applied, in most cases verbally, to the life of someone who has strayed from God's way. That person needs a corrective word to bring him back to the path of righteousness. When children sin, they need to know that it is also God who is displeased or dishonored, not just Mom or Dad. Next, children need to see that the ultimate answer when they sin is to obey God's Word, whether that means obeying His specific commands or keeping the fifth commandment by honoring their father and mother. Verbal correction affirms that the only way to find the "correct" path is by obeying God's Word and doing His will.

Finally, verbal correction has a greater impact when parents practice effective communication skills. What follows are several ways you can skillfully apply verbal discipline when you need to correct your child.

Speak the Truth in Love

Christ told his disciples that one of the ways the world would know they were His followers was by their "love for one another" (John 13:35). Any anger, harshness, or arguing in a body of believers prevents the world from seeing Christ there. The world sees Christ when the fruit of the Spirit is evident—love, joy, peace, patience, and the rest (see Galatians 5:22-23).

The same holds true for a Christian family. When the world hears parents yelling at their children, or being harsh and angry, or making them feel guilty, these nonbelievers are not seeing Christ in that family. How you correct your child will reflect Christ's presence—or absence—in your parenting.

When my family was acting in a major Christian musical production, I became aware of something in the Gospels that I'd never noticed before, probably because I was now *hearing* the Word spoken by an actor playing Christ. (Cast as a Pharisee, I was on the receiving end of some of Christ's words.) When Jesus spoke to the scribes and Pharisees, to those whose hearts were hardened, He spoke strong words with strong emotions. He was harsh, and He spoke with judgment. But when Jesus spoke to those who were following Him, those whose hearts were soft and open, He spoke gently and kindly.

Many Christian parents, myself included, tend to speak to children as though they were Pharisees. We can speak harshly and with judgment, implying by our manner that their hearts are hard and resistant. But this attitude is not justified by Scripture. There is no record of Jesus ever speaking to a child in a harsh tone. When the Gospels record Him speaking to a child, it is always with gentleness. Our children are not our adversaries. Though our children's hearts are corrupted by sin, they are not hardened sinners who have made conscious choices to reject the Savior. Our children are simply immature and childish. That's why children need love and compassion, not harshness and guilt.

If you deliver the Word of God to your children wrapped in harshness, guilt, and anger, that's what they'll remember whenever the Word is opened to them in the future. In contrast, you can be controlled by the Holy Spirit when you speak the Word of God to discipline your children. When you speak the truth in love and by the power of the Holy Spirit, even to correct or reprove your children, you are releasing God's grace into their lives. When you choose to speak a word of correction gently rather than harshly, you are telling your children that you know their hearts are open to you and to God.

Assume Your Biblical Authority

Jesus was unlike the other Jewish rabbis of His time, speaking by His own authority and not on the authority of others (see Matthew 7:28-29). Imagine the power of His words—in a field, on the street, or in a synagogue—whether He offered encouragement, rebuke, or instruction. Jesus didn't have to demand respect or submission to His authority because His authority came from God.

As a parent, you have God-given authority on three counts. First, with your own children, God has given you authority to "bring them up in…the Lord" (Ephesians 6:4). Children are, by God's design, already open to your influence and your God-given authority. Second, the fifth commandment, "Honor your father and your mother" (Exodus 20:12), delegates you authority over your children. Your children need to understand the nature of that authority. Third and most important, when you speak the Word of God into your child's heart and mind, you speak with God's authority. You are not speaking, but God is, and you have the authority of God Himself when His words are spoken through you.

When you verbally correct your child with the Word of God, don't mumble about not understanding everything about it, but rather speak the Word directly and confidently. Don't give your child the impression that the Bible is just another book by quoting it glibly or without conviction.

A caveat is important, though. Jesus was clear that the authority His followers were to exercise was to be characterized by service and not by positional power like the worldly rulers who would lord it over their subjects (see

Matthew 20:25-28). Parental authority when correcting your children is not an exercise in power and control, but an expression of service. You are serving your children by being Christ to them, by bringing them the life-changing Word of God.

Apply God's Word

When you need to correct your child, consider what kind of biblical input is needed. A useful grid is found in 2 Timothy 3:16: Does my child need instruction, or a reproving word about a particular sin, or a corrective word about what to do about that sin, or a disciplining (training) word about how to choose the path of righteousness?[3] As you observe the issues that come up in your child's life, make reference notes in the back of your Bible.

When you apply a scripture, make it personal for your child. Occasionally, you can send your child off to look up scriptures and report back to you. Better, though, is to say something like the following: "I want us to look up a scripture together and see what God has to say about your attitude. After you look up Philippians 2:3-4, let's read it together out loud." There will be times when you assign your child some Bible research as part of corrective discipline, but it's always better to do it together. It gives you an opportunity to have your child verbalize back to you what he's read, which helps him internalize the truth. You'll also have the chance to ask what he believes it means, which shows how he synthesizes it. And you can talk with him about what he should do, which personalizes the scripture for him. The process affirms your authority as well as God's authority in his life.

Whenever you use a scripture to correct your children, always find a way to apply it to them personally. They can hear it and know that God said it, but when it is applied, God has said it to *them*.

Express a Positive Message

Paul was a great motivator. In the first chapter of his letter to the Philippians, we find a pattern that can be labeled with the letters ACE. First, Paul expressed "affirmation" (see verses 3-6), identifying the positive things he saw in the lives of the Philippian Christians. Then he expressed "confirmation" (see verses 7-8) of his love for and commitment to them. Finally, he expressed "expectation" (see verses 9-11) of their response and growth in Christ.

The ACE acronym gives us a great way to think about what to say when we verbally discipline our children. Following the ACE pattern will also strengthen the bond of love with our children and will underscore our authority in their lives, especially if we use Scripture. First, we need to affirm the good things we see in our children's lives, the biblical character qualities that are strengths for them. They will realize that we see more in them than just the problem or the sin. Then, we confirm our love for them and our commitment to be a good and loving parent. We let them know that correction doesn't affect our relationships with them. Finally, we express an expectation of what we believe can happen in their lives. We let our children know that we see potential for what God can do in and through them.

When we verbally correct and discipline our child, even with the most loving and sympathetic spirit, we are delivering a message that is intrinsically negative. A child internalizes these words and probably also feels he has failed. We can't avoid the negative impact of verbal correction, but we can counterbalance it with an ACE message. Then our child will hear the negative correction but also the positive expressions.

Seek a Biblical Response

Most verbal correction addresses a problem but goes no further. For example: "Meredith, stop that right now! I don't like it when you're mean to your brother." We need to change the way we use verbal correction to make it solution-centered rather than problem-centered. To do so, we need to look beyond the immediate problem to the biblical response that will move a child in the right direction. A solution-centered correction might sound like this: "Meredith, I want you to stop being mean to your brother right

now. Meanness is the opposite of love, and it demonstrates a sinful attitude
that displeases God. You need to confess that sin to God and then ask your
brother for forgiveness to restore your relationship." That's an overly abbreviated example, but you get the idea.

There are a great many biblical responses that can help you correct
your child. Here are some of the more common responses.

- *Confession:* "If we confess our sins, He is faithful and righteous
  to forgive us our sins and to cleanse us from all unrighteousness"
  (1 John 1:9). Whenever you verbally correct your child, you should
  also seek a response of confession, which simply means to "agree
  with God" about the sin. You can insist that your child cease from
  a particular sin, but only confession insures that your child owns
  the sin.

- *Forgiveness:* "Be kind to one another, tender-hearted, forgiving
  each other, just as God in Christ also has forgiven you" (Ephesians
  4:32). If you have more than one child, many of their sins will be
  committed against one another. Just as sin has broken the relationship between God and humankind, it also breaks the relationship
  between child and child. Forgiveness is the only way to restore the
  relationship. If Christ forgives us, then we must forgive one
  another. Correction is incomplete without restoration.

- *Repentance:* "The Lord is not slow about His promise, as some
  count slowness, but is patient toward you, not wishing for any to
  perish but for all to come to repentance" (2 Peter 3:9). Repentance
  means to change your mind about sin. Verbal correction assumes
  your child understands that there needs to be a change of mind,
  but that change doesn't happen until your child actually renounces
  his sin and turns from it. This is a necessary response for trouble-
  some sin that has become a habit.

- *Conviction:* "And He [the Holy Spirit], when He comes, will convict the world concerning sin and righteousness and judgment"

(John 16:8). Conviction is the internal recognition of sin. When you verbally correct your child, it is with the intent that the Holy Spirit will use your words to convict your child's heart concerning the sin that is being corrected.

- *Godly sorrow:* "For the sorrow that is according to the will of God produces a repentance without regret, leading to salvation, but the sorrow of the world produces death" (2 Corinthians 7:10). Godly sorrow, like conviction, is an internal recognition of sin that results in sorrow for having offended God. This is probably a more mature response to sin, but even a younger child who is corrected can feel this sorrow. If he has committed a serious sin (relative to childhood), godly sorrow may be an appropriate response to seek from your child.

Verbal Discipline on the Path of Life

To ignore a behavior that needs correction is to condone it, so you can't remain silent when you see a sinful action or attitude. Your children need to hear through your spoken words and in your tone of voice that they have sinned. The most effective form of verbal discipline includes the Word of God so that your child knows he is accountable not just to you, but also to God. It's your responsibility both to bring Scripture into your verbal discipline and to apply it to your child's life in a mature way.

Paul told Timothy in the closing words of his last letter, "Preach the word; be ready in season and out of season; reprove, rebuke, exhort, with great patience and instruction" (2 Timothy 4:2). I find this charge appropriate not just for a pastor, but also for every Christian parent. God calls me to be ready, in season and out, to bring the Word of God to bear on my children's lives. I must proclaim God's Word to my children all the time and everywhere we are (see Deuteronomy 6:7). I am called to use the Word of God to reprove (correct) my children, rebuke their sin, and exhort them to obey Him. Such discipline requires me to be patient with my children's immaturity, knowing that growth sometimes comes slowly. It's also a task that requires me to know God's Word so that I can instruct my children in its truths. And, lest you missed it, Paul's charge to Timothy was entirely verbal. It's an example of the type of verbal discipline that my children need in the process of corrective discipline.

BEHAVIORAL DISCIPLINE

Using Consequences to Shape a Child's Will

S usan, I noticed that your bed wasn't made again this morning. I know you had plenty of time, so I was wondering why that didn't get done."

"Oh, Mom, it's too hard to get everything done in the morning. I get dressed, eat breakfast, we start talking, and I just forget."

"I know you're busy. But what did we decide about making your bed?"

"That if I didn't make my bed, I'd have to wash five windows. Are you really going to make me do that?"

"Well, I wouldn't want you to think it's okay not to follow through on doing what you say you're going to do. You *chose* to wash the windows when you failed to make your bed. Don't do the bed; do the windows. You actually made that decision earlier this morning."

Susan did the windows—and she did so with a good attitude. Her mother's reminder of the agreement they'd made helped Susan take responsibility for her failure to make her bed and to bear the consequences of her decision.

CHOICES AND CONSEQUENCES

One of the most basic lessons that our children need to learn early in life is that choices have consequences. Big choices, little choices, innocent choices, impulsive choices—like the law of action and reaction, every choice has a consequence. And we have to live with the consequence. Proverbs is really a book about choices and consequences, about making wise choices rather than foolish ones in order to experience positive consequences rather than negative ones.

When the Israelites were about to enter the Promised Land, Moses read the Law with the reminder that blessings follow obedience and a curse follows disobedience. In the New Testament, Paul says, "Do not be deceived, God is not mocked; for whatever a man sows, this he will also reap. For the one who sows to his own flesh will from the flesh reap corruption, but the one who sows to the Spirit will from the Spirit reap eternal life" (Galatians 6:7-8). The Bible is all about choices and consequences.

When most parents hear the word *consequences* in the context of discipline, they naturally think of negative consequences. And as we discuss corrective discipline, we recognize that the natural consequences of unwise choices are negative. However, an approach to discipline that offers only negative consequences is woefully incomplete. Positive consequences, or incentives, should also be a core component of a parent's discipline plan. Even the nature of a person's choices about God includes incentives (heaven, eternal rewards) and disincentives (hell, eternal separation from God). This picture of how God deals with humanity can serve as a guide for us as we deal with our children.

Incentives attach a reward (such as money, a treat, or a special privilege) to a responsibility or chore (such as taking out the trash). This adds a positive motivation, even if just for a brief time. Incentives are not always effective when dealing with virtue-related character issues such as love, honesty, or self-control, but they can, if used wisely, provide positive motivations for your children to be more responsible. Some parents fear that incentives train children to do good only because they are seeking a payment, rather than being motivated by an intrinsic desire to do good. On the other hand, a small incentive is a reminder that good choices are often rewarded in life.

Scripture teaches that we reap what we sow, both good and bad. There is no general rule about incentives that will apply to all children in every family, so follow the Spirit's leading. Use discernment as to what kind of incentive will be right for each of your children.

Since we are dealing with corrective discipline, consider now the use of disincentives to correct a child's misbehavior, bad attitudes, or irresponsibility. If your verbal correction has failed to generate the desired response, then it may be time to employ behavioral correction, which involves establishing consequences for certain behaviors. The goal of behavioral discipline is to make your child accountable for his choices and decisions. Instead of being arbitrary punishment meted out according to a parent's whims, consequences make the correction a discipline that is "chosen" by the child. It teaches a child the reality of the "if…then" equation: The choices he makes determine the consequences he experiences.

Corrective discipline employs two kinds of consequences: natural and logical. Natural consequences follow foolish or willful wrong behavior when there has been no prior agreement between you and your child concerning that behavior. You support the natural consequence or impose one that seems "natural" and fitting to the offense. A simple example would be a child with an ice cream cone foolishly turning the cone upside down to see if the ice cream would stick to the cone, or running around with the cone and having the ice cream fall to the ground. Rather than replace the ice cream, a wise parent will use this natural consequence for instruction: "I'm sorry that happened, Sean. I know how much you like ice cream, and seeing it drop on the ground would disappoint me, too. I hope you'll be more careful the next time." The correction is delivered with sympathy and without guilt or shame. But the consequence is allowed to do its work.

Another example of a natural consequence would be what happens when two sisters knock over a lamp while fighting over a toy. A natural consequence would be to deduct the cost of the lamp from their future allowance, or perhaps to have the girls do extra work to pay for replacing the lamp. Utilize a consequence that is natural to the offense, not one that seems completely disconnected from it. Natural consequences can be applied to a wide range of behavioral problems, using a variety of consequences such as time outs, loss of privileges, and additional household chores. This type of consequence allows the parent to address a behavioral issue at the time it occurs and in a way that will make a point.

Logical consequences, on the other hand, involve a prior agreement between parent and child concerning particular behaviors, such as Susan's failure to make her bed. She had to wash five windows since that was the agreed-upon consequence of failing to make her bed. Another example might be a child who has developed the habit of saying unkind words to a sibling. The agreed-upon logical consequence might be something as simple, when it happens, as writing out ten times a Bible verse about controlling one's tongue or about being kind. Another scenario might involve chores or responsibilities that are not performed as agreed. In that case, the child knows ahead of time that additional chores will be required. It's almost like a contract that you and your child settle on. Whatever the logical consequence might be, the goal is to make your children personally accountable for their actions. It's not simply a matter of the parent imposing discipline. Instead, the children are choosing to suffer the agreed-upon consequence because they chose to disobey.

This kind of behavioral discipline begins as soon as a child can understand what you are saying, and it continues throughout childhood: "If you leave your toys on the floor, then you won't be allowed to play with them for a week. If you don't complete your assignment for school, then you won't be allowed to go on the field trip." When you establish a clear consequence ahead of time, you're encouraging your children to take personal responsibility for their behavior.

Discipline That Works on a Child's Will

The key to behavioral discipline is consistency. It's like a diet. If you're not consistent in saying no to chocolate bars, you'll soon be saying yes all the time. Consistency, though, strengthens the will. The more you exercise the will to say no, the stronger your will becomes and the more consistent you'll become. Since childhood discipline is all about "will training," you're using behavioral discipline to help your children strengthen their will.

Sally and I use from Proverbs 20:11 to remind our children that what they do defines who they are in other people's eyes: "Even a child is known by his actions, by whether his conduct is pure and right" (NIV). Actions speak louder than words, even when it comes to a child's reputation. To be exegetically honest, I should disclose that the "child" here is a *naar*, which has a teenage son in view, but the principle still holds true for younger children.

But there is more to that verse than immediately meets the eye. Here it is in a slight paraphrase: "Even a child's training is revealed by his actions, by whether he has been trained to choose what is pure and right." Your children's actions say as much about your consistency in training as they do about your children's character. Christian education pioneer H. Clay Trumbull said: "It is, therefore, largely a child's training that settles the question [of what kind of person he will become].... In all these things his course indicates what his training has been; or it suggests the training that he needed, but missed."[1]

The great challenge for parents is to stay consistent in training a child's will. The ultimate goal of childhood discipline is to strengthen a child's will to say no to sin and yes to what is pure and right. That is the ministry of grace in their lives, and you are the channel. Training the will reaches into a child's heart and spirit, where God is at work through His Spirit. That means that strengthening a child's will, as part of a parent's biblical job description, is a spiritual task. It requires the parent to be walking consistently in the power of the Spirit. The more consistently you walk in the Spirit, the more consistently you will exercise, with grace, corrective discipline. Your consistent and gracious corrective discipline will strengthen your child's will to choose healthy godliness rather than chocolaty sin in the future.

The converse is also true. The less consistently you walk with Christ, the less consistently you will train your child's will and the more you will weaken it, encouraging him by your inaction to choose what comes easily or naturally. Or, if you are harsh and strict, only concerned about controlling your child's misbehavior, he will learn to say no only to avoid punishment, but not to say yes because he wants to choose good. Training your children to walk confidently on the path of life with you requires consistent heartfelt involvement in their lives.

According to Proverbs 29:15, "A child who gets his own way brings shame to his mother." The problem is not the child, but the child "who gets his own way." The alternate reading in Hebrew, "a child left to himself," suggests that the real problem is the parent. This is a child whose will-training has been neglected and who ends up leaving the path of life and going his own way. A child won't automatically heed his parents' correction. We must instruct and correct a child so he will know how to choose the path of wisdom.

THE ELEMENTS OF BEHAVIORAL DISCIPLINE

A child can understand consequences when they are presented in a simple statement: "If you do that, then you will suffer this unpleasant outcome." The goal is not to control but to lovingly train a child's will to help her grow in maturity. Heartfelt discipline would never issue the ultimatum: "If you do that one more time, you'll regret it!"

Dr. Ross Campbell describes two kinds of parents in his book *Relational Parenting*. He says that parents who practice "reactive" parenting respond primarily to what their children do; those who practice "proactive" parenting deal primarily with what their children need. He wrote, "The reactive approach results in punishment-oriented parenting. The proactive approach anticipates and then seeks to meet the most basic needs of children. This positive, proactive approach is the more effective way to rear children. To consistently express love for the child is the basis of effective parenting."[2]

Heartfelt discipline helps you create a loving, heart-to-heart relationship with your children that lets them know you're on their side and that, when corrective discipline is called for, you are trying to help them become more mature. Their heart need, as children, is not to be punished and controlled but to be helped and directed to experience the blessings of choosing God's way. Paul told us that this is what biblical love does: "As a result, we are no longer to be children, tossed here and there by waves and carried about by every wind of doctrine, by the trickery of men, by craftiness in deceitful scheming; but speaking the truth in love, we are to grow up in all aspects into Him who is the head, even Christ" (Ephesians 4:14-15). Our children are not yet mature, and they need us to "speak the truth in love" so they can grow up in Christ.

As you use the tools of natural consequences and logical consequences, the question is how to keep them heartfelt and directed at your child's real needs. If you understand what it means to live in the power of the Holy Spirit, your behavioral discipline—discipline by faith—will meet your child's heartfelt needs. If you discipline by the flesh or by formula, you'll miss your child's needs. How you use behavioral discipline will determine whether it's a ministry of grace or an application of the Law. Here are some issues to consider as you make behavioral discipline a part of your heartfelt relationship with your children.

Honor

There is really only one direct command in Scripture that addresses children. The fifth of God's ten commandments says, "Honor your father and your mother, as the LORD your God has commanded you, that your days may be prolonged and that it may go well with you on the land which the LORD your God gives you" (Deuteronomy 5:16, reaffirmed in Ephesians 6:1-3 and Colossians 3:20). The only commandment directed to children has a consequence attached to it, or in this case an incentive. Thus, God affirms behavioral discipline in the Ten Commandments!

I like to think that the fifth commandment is the hinge between the first four about honoring God and the last five about honoring others. Without it, we can't open the door to God's blessings. Jesus said that the greatest commandment is to "love the Lord your God," and the second one is to "love your neighbor" (Matthew 22:37-39). If a person refuses to honor his parents, how can he honor God and others? That is why honor is so critical in behavioral discipline. Honoring parents is a child's path to fulfilling the law of love.

Here's another crucial aspect of honor: It's a two-way street. Your children are commanded to honor you, but it is from you that they learn what honor means. By your words and actions, they will see how you honor your own parents, God, and other people, and, closer to home, how you honor them. Scripture says we are to "honor all people," which certainly includes our children (1 Peter 2:17).

The primary words used for *honor* in both the Old and New Testaments have similar meanings. The Hebrew word is associated with "weightiness." The weightier a person, the more worthy or valued he is and the more deserving of honor. The Greek word can also convey the idea of "value" or "worth," as in fixing a price. When your children honor you, they are acknowledging your "weight" in God's eyes (that would be your *spiritual* weight) and your intrinsic "value." When you honor your children, you are acknowledging their importance and value to you and to God. If your discipline doesn't affirm that you see your children as incredibly worthy and valued, then it lacks honor. Honor and grace go hand in hand in corrective discipline. When you honor your children's value in God's eyes, you also extend His grace to them.

Note, however, that children are never instructed to fear their parents as one would fear God. We fear God because we know that we deserve His judgment and punishment because of our sin. However, if you believe that effective parenting requires you to instill fear of your punishment in your children, then you need to reexamine your understanding of biblical love. John, the apostle of love, says, "There is no fear in love; but perfect love casts out fear, because fear involves punishment, and the one who fears is not perfected in love" (1 John 4:18). When you honor your children and recognize their worth in God's eyes, you are freeing them from fear so that they can respond to your love and learn how to give honor back to you.

When you exercise behavioral discipline, do so with the goal of honoring your children's worth and value. There simply is no reason to make them feel unworthy in order to correct them. The Holy Spirit will convict as needed. When your children see you honor them, they will learn how to honor you.[3]

Obedience

Obedience is really an aspect of children's honoring their parents. Paul instructed the Ephesians, "Children, *obey* your parents in the Lord, for this is right," quoting the fifth commandment along with a parenthetical reminder that it is "the first commandment with a promise" (6:1-3). He also said to the Colossians, "Children, *be obedient* to your parents in all things, for this is well-pleasing to the Lord" (3:20). Obedience is both "right" and "well-pleasing" to God because it honors parents. But Paul also described what kind of obedience is commanded. First, your children should obey you "in the Lord" (Ephesians 6:1). This statement acknowledges that children can relate to you on a spiritual level. However, it's your responsibility to keep your parenting "of the Lord" (Ephesians 6:4) so that your children will be able to respond "in the Lord." Second, obedience is to be "in all things" (Colossians 3:20). Paul was simply acknowledging that obedience is not an option for children; it's a command. There is no area of life exempt from your child's responsibility to obey you. Children need to learn to honor God by honoring their parents, the human authorities God has placed over them.

Obedience and honor are really two sides of the same coin. It's all too easy to fall into a pattern of insisting on obedience, but not on honor. The result is that you might be able to make a child stop a wrong or unwanted behavior, but your child may still dishonor you in his heart by frowning, pouting, or sulking. Without requiring honor, you will train your children in the way of superficial obedience that teaches them to comply outwardly, and you'll never confront their inward attitudes. Heartfelt discipline, as its name suggests, reaches the heart level to secure not just a child's obedience but also his respect. As obedience speaks to actions, then honor speaks to attitudes, and when you use the tool of behavioral discipline your goal is to correct both actions and attitudes.

Attitudes, though, generally respond more slowly than actions. So you will be called upon to exercise patience. Not every situation needs to become a "because I'm the parent, that's why" showdown or shutdown. Some besetting sins will take a little longer to train out of your children. Keep your focus on your child's heart, not just on the behavior. At the same time, be sensitive to issues of age, personality, circumstances, and immaturity that can affect your child's obedience. Don't expect sterling obedience and respectful attitudes when your child is tired, hungry, or overstimulated. All disobedience is not the same, and you need to be sensitive to your child's real needs.

Heart

Your child's heart needs to be your focus. When practicing behavioral discipline, you are naturally focused on behavior just as you focus on the image in the foreground when you're using binoculars. Before doing anything, though, you need to manually refocus the lens of your spirit until your child's heart in the background comes into clear view.

In the Bible, the word *heart* is used most often to describe the inner person, the spiritual dimension of our being. It's the part that is in touch with eternity and that connects with the Savior. It is the source of our emotions, our drives, our motives, our intentions. It is the control center of our lives. You can't ignore your child's heart.

How often have you noticed an angry child become quiet and relaxed as a parent touches her head, speaks gently, and takes time to hear her child's immature but very real frustrations? A child confesses and discusses the problem calmly and sensibly as a parent takes time to talk, listen, counsel, and read Scripture. Feuding siblings talk to one another and ask forgiveness because their parents made the effort to talk calmly and firmly about the heart issues of love, kind words, and forgiveness.

THE BOTTOM LINE ON BEHAVIORAL DISCIPLINE

It's far too easy for parents to misuse behavioral discipline as a tool for control. So be sure you're walking in the grace of God when you correct your children. It's natural to want to respond to misbehavior and bad attitudes with rigid law—to make your children feel guilty, cower them with your anger, lord your parental power over them. However, it is *super*natural to respond to them in grace—to sympathize, love them, honor them, serve them. You might be thinking, "Oh, come on. You don't know my kids! I need to be strict, or I'll completely lose control." It's true that I don't know your children, but I do know that the picture of God we have in the Bible is our paradigm for relating to our children in grace. Paul said, "But when the *kindness* of God our Savior and His *love* for mankind appeared, He saved us, not on the basis of deeds which we have done in righteousness, but according to His *mercy*...so that being justified by His *grace* we would be made heirs according to the *hope* of eternal life" (Titus 3:4-7). When we deserved His grace the least, that's when God gave it to us.

This is the faith part of disciplining our children. You choose to rely on the ministry of the Holy Spirit in your life to give you wisdom to discipline your children, rather than relying on a formula or resorting to the imposition of law. You choose to believe that you can trust the power of God's grace to work in your children's hearts, rather than relying on harshness and strictness to control your children. When you correct your children using the tool of behavioral discipline, you focus on their hearts, not just on their behaviors. When you focus on the heart, you're working where God is at work, shaping your children for His purposes.

CHAPTER 12

PHYSICAL DISCIPLINE

Correction That Works on a Child's "Won't"

It sure seemed like the normal thing to do. When Sarah was just a toddler, she reached for an electrical outlet. Being a conscientious dad, I let
out an authoritative "NO!" and slapped her sweet, chubby little hand. She
wailed and pouted a bit, but was soon off exploring again. I watched for
several days to see if she would return to the electrical outlet, and she never
again reached for it (at least in my presence). I thought, *Hey, that little hand
slap sure worked well*, and figured I'd found the way to go.

As Sarah got older and her behavior became more challenging at times,
I moved on to bottom swats, finding that they also seemed to work, at least
most of the time. The initial swats with a hand eventually progressed to a
kitchen spatula or whatever item that resembled a paddle was handy. Sally
and I weren't mean or excessive by any stretch. We were just trying to do
what seemed best to train our daughter, and spanking seemed to come
naturally.

But it soon became clear that spanking wasn't always the easy answer
we had come to think it was. When Sarah was young, there were occasional
and sometimes inexplicable battles of the will. From our reading of Christian books on discipline, we were convinced that we had to win these battles.
Rather than ending the battle, though, spanking often seemed only to
make the situation worse, sometimes even escalating the conflict. Those
times left me wondering if I was missing something.

With twenty-twenty hindsight, I now realize that spanking was never the only option and rarely the best option. In many cases, Sarah needed to be distracted, put to bed, or loved and given some grace. She was just a little girl with a child's curiosity but without an adult's practiced judgment. It was unreasonable for me to expect an adult level of self-control from a child, but I didn't see that at the time. Spanking was what I knew to do, others were saying it worked, and Scripture seemed to endorse physical punishment, so I felt I was on pretty safe ground.

Today, though, after four children, eighteen years of parenting experience, and a better understanding of Scripture, I probably would never use physical discipline as I did back then. It's not God's mandated method as I once thought. I don't believe spanking children is prohibited by Scripture, but I've learned gentler ways to achieve the same results. The gentler way of heartfelt discipline takes into account God's view of children and the way He wants parents to view their children. And it brings to bear God's grace, our faith, and the leading of the Holy Spirit on the nurture and discipline of our children.

A NEW LOOK AT PHYSICAL DISCIPLINE

Physical discipline isn't limited to a hand slap or the use of a rod or paddle. It can also include rapping the knuckles, pinching a shoulder (or ear lobe), and other similar physical acts. It's anything that causes a child physical discomfort or pain in an effort to get his attention or respond to his inappropriate behavior or attitude. By nature it is punitive.

Some argue that physical discipline doesn't always have to be punitive. Because it is God's mandated method of discipline, they argue, it is always training in righteousness (turning a child from sin to God), not punishment. I disagree. Any deliberate action by a parent meant to inflict pain or discomfort on a child in response to undesirable behavior is punishment. It may have the effect of training, but the act itself, by its nature, is punitive. Physical discipline is really the ultimate form of behavioral discipline; it is the most serious consequence parents can impose as a part of corrective discipline. If it is perceived as a form of positive training methodology, then it actually fits into the behavior-modification system developed by B. F. Skinner and other behavioral psychologists. Spanking is negative reinforcement (pain) that produces a desired response (compliance) from the child. My first inclination is to reject that approach out of hand, but I can't deny God's use of physical discipline as punishment. He is not opposed to it on principle, but as we have seen in previous chapters, Scripture never associates the use of the rod with children—only with young men, adults, and nations.

Scripture is filled with examples of God's punishment of His people through suffering and persecution. Though loved and guided by God, the nation of Israel was on the receiving end of His rod of correction and His hand of judgment when they disobeyed.[1] Even those who love and obey God are not exempt from physical discipline that is meant to make them more mature.[2] But this kind of discipline in Scripture is always directed toward adults, never small children. Children may suffer secondarily when God punishes adults, but His judgment is aimed squarely at those who are morally culpable. And as we have seen in previous chapters, children younger than a certain age don't fit that profile.

This biblical background leaves Christian parents asking a crucial question: What role *does* physical discipline play in the biblical discipline of young children? When, if ever, should a Christian parent use physical punishment, for what infractions, and at what age? These are valid questions, but they are not answered directly by Scripture. The rod passages of Proverbs, as we saw in chapter 3, have young men in view, not young children. Those passages speak of the physical discipline of young adults and adults (beating them on the backs with rods), so we cannot draw from those scriptures any principle that applies to the physical discipline of children.

The teaching of Scripture, then, brings us back to parenting by faith, the basis of heartfelt discipline. God expects us to follow our redeemed, Spirit-led instincts when it comes to using physical discipline on our children. Without a divine mandate to follow, parents must seek God's will and pray to hear Him accurately in order to determine what is right for their own family. If you decide to use physical discipline, do so out of personal conviction that the Holy Spirit has directed you to, not out of an incomplete reading of Scripture or an unexamined commitment to someone else's views.

GUIDANCE FROM THE NEW TESTAMENT

There is an instructive passage in 1 Corinthians that provides a rare glimpse into Paul's views on the physical discipline of children. Paul was writing to the troubled church in Corinth to address problems of factions and immorality, among other things. This young, very immature body of believers was disobedient, disorderly, and badly in need of discipline. Paul wrote to reprove and correct them.

He described his relationship to this childish church when he said, "I do not write these things to shame you, but to admonish you as my beloved children" (4:14). They certainly deserved to feel some shame over their arrogance about incest, but Paul did not give them a guilt trip. Instead, he wrote to admonish them as his children. This is the same word (*noutheteo*) Paul used in Ephesians when he told fathers to bring up their children in the "discipline and *instruction*" of the Lord. He then called himself a father to the Corinthian Christians: "For if you were to have countless tutors in Christ, yet you would not have many fathers, for in Christ Jesus I became your father through the gospel" (4:15). The word *tutors* means a "teacher of boys" and is the same root of the term for "discipline." Paul was making the comparison to family very clear: His heart for the Corinthians was the same as a father's who sees his young son's needing discipline and instruction in the Lord.

Paul then pointed out that the real issue in discipline is spiritual power, not personal power or control over our children. In confronting the errors in the Corinthian church, Paul reminded them that "the kingdom of God does not consist in words but in power" (4:20). In other words, the power of men's words is nothing compared to the power of the Holy Spirit when it corrects sin. Paul was confident of the Holy Spirit's power to prevail. It is no different with parenting: The Holy Spirit is the real source of effectiveness in our discipline.

At this point, Paul provided the only New Testament reference to the rod as an instrument of personal discipline. Elsewhere in the New Testament, *rods* refers to scepters and staffs and as instruments of divine judgment. Paul was even beaten with rods. But only in the 1 Corinthians passage does the rod of Proverbs appear in the hands of a father who needs to discipline his children. This word *rhabdos* is the Greek word the Jews used to translate the Hebrew word *shebet,* found in Proverbs.

Paul asked the Corinthian believers: "What do you desire? Shall I come to you with a rod, or with love and a spirit of gentleness?" (4:21). The rhetorical nature of the question is clear. Paul was not really offering them a choice, but telling them his intentions. Despite his natural inclination to go and knock some sense into them, Paul knew that the correct spiritual response was to confront them "with love and a spirit of gentleness." If he had made that point without reference to his father-child relationship to them, we might miss the connection. But Paul drew the lines of comparison very clearly, giving us a brief glimpse into his view of physical discipline within the family.

The love that guided Paul's discipline was, of course, *agape* love—the unconditional, sacrificial, selfless love that moved God to send His Son to die for us, the kind of love that Christ said should be the hallmark of His disciples, and the kind of love that Paul taught as the supreme virtue and motivation of every Christian. Paul went on in this letter to describe that love as "patient [and] kind" (1 Corinthians 13:4). It's the kind of love you have for your children. But Paul took the contrast with the rod one step further by adding that he would come with "a spirit of gentleness." This gentleness defines how he would relate to the Corinthians and how he pictured a father would relate to his own child. Gentleness is the controlling motivation and could even be said, along with love, to be the power of the Spirit that Paul would bring. It is, after all, a fruit of the Holy Spirit mentioned in Galatians 5:23.

When I looked at gentleness as it appears in other passages, I was surprised by its connection with discipline:

Take My yoke upon you and learn from Me, for I am *gentle* and *humble in heart,* and you will find rest for your souls (Matthew 11:29).

Jesus had just pronounced judgment on cities that had rejected His miracles, but in His invitation to those who will follow Him, He said that He was gentle and meek.

Brethren, even if anyone is caught in any trespass, you who are spiritual, *restore* such a one *in a spirit of gentleness.* (Galatians 6:1)

Correction and restoration are to be done, as in Corinth, by the power of the Spirit and with a spirit of gentleness.

But we proved to be *gentle* among you, as a nursing mother tenderly cares for her own children (1 Thessalonians 2:7).

Gentleness is characteristic of the kind of parental love Paul showed the church.

The Lord's bond-servant must not be quarrelsome, but be *kind to all,* able to teach, patient when wronged, *with gentleness correcting those who are in opposition,* if perhaps God may grant them repentance leading to the knowledge of the truth." (2 Timothy 2:24-25)

In other words, Timothy should be gentle even with those who oppose him.

Paul clearly rejected a harsh, judgmental correction associated with the rod, even for a church that appeared to deserve it. Instead, he promoted a loving, gentle correction. But what about Hebrews 12:1-11, the clearest expression of fatherly discipline in the New Testament? That passage seems to teach physical discipline. It helps to keep in mind that, first of all, like the young man of Proverbs, the child in view here is an older child, a teenager. The author of Hebrews (probably not Paul) quoted Proverbs 3:11-12, which is about the *naar,* or young man, responding to God's discipline and reproof. The author, though, added a word to the Proverbs passage in the final line that raises the issue of physical discipline: "FOR THOSE WHOM THE LORD LOVES HE DISCIPLINES, AND HE *SCOURGES* EVERY SON WHOM HE RECEIVES" (12:6). The term *scourges* means "to whip" and is the same word used to describe the scourging Jesus received by Pilate. The question, then, is why the inspired author of Hebrews added this word. It is clearly not there, nor even implied, in the Proverbs text.

In the previous chapter, the writer had just listed Israel's Hall of Faith, including some believers who "experienced...scourgings" (11:36) and were still faithful. The Christians reading the letter, though, those scattered after the persecutions in Jerusalem, had not yet "resisted to the point of shedding blood in your striving against sin" (12:4), and the author wanted to emphasize to them that God does sometimes "discipline" His children with painful suffering and even death, so he added the word *scourges.* It is, he said, a mark of our sonship as children of God. He likened God's discipline of His people to the kind of discipline that all sons have received from fathers. It is not altogether clear that the "earthly fathers" mentioned here are godly fathers, since they are contrasted with the heavenly Father who disciplines "for our good, so that we may share His holiness," but the parallel to parenting is clear (12:10).

The real point of the Hebrews passage is the writer's conclusion: "All discipline for the moment seems not to be joyful, but sorrowful; yet to those who have been trained by it, afterwards it yields the peaceful fruit of righteousness" (12:11). Even hard discipline, physical discipline, will yield a good fruit. However, the context of this passage prevents us from making it a case for physical discipline of young children. It isn't.

WHERE DO WE GO FROM HERE?

Paul said, "Be imitators of me, just as I also am of Christ" (1 Corinthians 11:1). Your children are your disciples, so part of your responsibility is to model for them the character of Christ. Your children will learn what He is like from your example, and they will want to become like the Christ they see in you. Physical discipline is not a part of the biblical portrait of the Savior. There is good reason that you should find it difficult to imagine Jesus raising His hand to strike a child in punishment. It would contradict the biblical portrait of Jesus as the loving Savior and the gentle Shepherd, laying hands on the children to bless them. But a punitive Jesus is, in part, the picture you draw in your children's minds when you use physical discipline. No matter how loving you try to make it, in a day of "What Would Jesus Do?" it is hard to make the case that spanking is what Jesus would do.

My conclusion is this: Physical discipline of children is not mandated by Scripture or, for that matter, even modeled in Scripture. There really is no biblical basis for using physical discipline on young children. On the other hand, neither is there any biblical prohibition or direct condemnation of spanking. When the testimony of Scripture is either silent or inconclusive, we are left to listen to the testimony of the Holy Spirit to help us discern what is right, best, wisest, and most biblical. It's a matter of exercising our freedom in the Spirit to study the Scriptures, pray, and make a decision as to what is right.

That is the fleshing out of Paul's admonition: "The faith which you have, have as your own conviction before God. Happy is he who does not condemn himself in what he approves" (Romans 14:22). The issue is not about judging someone else's choices for disciplining their children, but about being convinced in our own spirits. We need to be settled and sure about what we have approved without thinking that we need to turn it into Christian law for others. "So then each one of us will give an account of himself to God. Therefore let us not judge one another anymore" (Romans 14:12-13).

It is my personal conviction that the radical teachings of Christ on love and forgiveness, and Paul's further teachings on grace and freedom, must be applied as seriously to childhood discipline as they are applied to relationships in the body of Christ. Jesus rebuked the Pharisees for failing to reflect God's heart in their application of the Law. But with His followers, He was compassionate and loving, not harsh and strict. Paul admonished Christians not to give up their freedom in Christ by creating "Christian law" for their lives and especially not to apply that law to others (see Galatians 5). We are freed from law, both the Old Testament Law and Christian legalism. We are to live by the power of the Holy Spirit, not by rules and regulations.

Let me throw out a few questions for you to ask as you search out your own heart on the issue of physical discipline.

- Are you ever more concerned about applying a disciplinary formula or method than you are about expressing God's heart to your children? Does the approach you follow reflect Christ's ways, and does it clearly and accurately give your children a picture of Christ's love and care?

- Are you free in the Spirit to follow the law of love with your children, or do you fall back on the false security of rules and regulations? Do you expect other Christians to apply those same rules within their families?

- Have you become so fearful of being permissive that you have lost the ability to simply trust in the power of God's love in your children's lives—in kindness, compassion, patience, and humility?
- Would you resist being known as a "gentle" disciplinarian simply because you are concerned about what "strict" disciplinarians would think? Are you afraid not to spank because of what it would do to your reputation?

DISCIPLINE THAT WORKS ON A CHILD'S "WON'T"

Knowing that most parents will, at times, use some form of physical discipline, let's consider some reasonable, commonsense guidelines for its use.[3] Obviously, the following are issues of wisdom and principle and not biblical mandates, since Scripture doesn't address the issue of physical discipline during childhood.

Punish with Physical Discipline Only When Necessary

It's easy to get into the habit of using physical discipline even though it may not be necessary or even warranted. If you have decided to use spanking, reserve it only for the most egregious offenses against your authority. If you have or do become accustomed to using it out of convenience rather than out of conviction, you should stop its use completely and reexamine your discipline. When you respond with physical discipline because it's "easier," or if you use it more and more for less serious offenses, you no longer have your child's good in mind but your own convenience.

Define in Advance Which Offenses Warrant Spanking

If your child senses that physical discipline is administered arbitrarily, you may be sowing seeds of anger and resentment. Clearly and prayerfully define with your child what kinds of sins or offenses will merit physical discipline. That way your child knows in advance and won't be surprised by a spanking.

Talk with Your Child Before You Administer Physical Discipline
Before a spanking, be sure your child knows why he is being disciplined and what he should expect. Ask your child to tell you which offense has led to physical discipline, so that he can acknowledge responsibility for both the offense and the consequence. Affirm your love for your child (if you can't, you are probably too angry and should delay your discipline). After the punishment, comfort your child, pray with him, encourage him to confess his sin to God, and steer him toward asking forgiveness of anyone he has hurt or offended. Before parting, affirm again your love for and confidence in your child.

Be Sensitive to Your Child's Limits
Know your child's threshold of discomfort and be careful not to exceed it. Physical discipline should never cause more than temporary discomfort. A few years back, one book on Christian discipline suggested that bruises from a spanking were not a big deal. We contacted the publisher, explaining that punishment that causes bruising is clearly excessive and could be reported as abuse. Although that passage was excised from later editions, it could not be excised from the minds of the many parents who read it. Other books talk about continuously spanking until the child completely surrenders (when the body muscles go limp) or about parents' making sure that the spanking is hard enough and lasts long enough to ensure its effectiveness. Nonsense! God has issued no such instructions, so know that any such "Christian" commentary on spanking is nothing more than personal opinion. In addition to your child's limits, you should also know your own so that your discipline is never in danger of becoming excessive, but instead is always measured, restrained, and controlled. Also, spanking on a bare bottom is both excessive and humiliating to a child. Don't do it.

Never Punish in Anger or in Haste

This guideline should not even need to be stated, but when a busy lifestyle allows little time for stopping, relating, and reaching your child's heart, physical discipline can easily become a quick and convenient way to stop an unwanted behavior. That means it is often used in haste, substituting for a preferred, but time-consuming, form of heartfelt discipline. Other times, spanking is used in anger because the parent acts out of emotion rather than according to the leading of the Holy Spirit. It's true in our discipline, as well as in our relationships, that "the anger of man does not achieve the righteousness of God" (James 1:20).

Punish Only in Private, Never in Public

If you choose to use physical discipline, never use it in public. At the very least, you risk damaging your Christian testimony in your community, especially if you become hasty or angry in your discipline. But there is an even more important reason to punish only in private, and that is to preserve your child's dignity. No matter how badly your child is behaving, you should never be guilty of publicly humiliating her. Go to another room, leave the restaurant, come back for your groceries, cancel plans—physical discipline should be administered without an audience. That also means without an audience of siblings, other children, or strangers.

PHYSICAL DISCIPLINE ON THE PATH OF LIFE

For many years I chose not to challenge the widely held view that physical discipline—spanking—is God's mandated method. Somewhere along the way, though, I took the time to carefully examine that view. When I found the Bible silent on the topic, I realized that the common practice of physical discipline is based on a misreading or misunderstanding of the message of four brief texts in the book of Proverbs and one other in the book of Hebrews. Simply put: Physical discipline of young children is not taught by Scripture. As we saw in chapter 3, there is no credible, defensible way to apply those passages directly or even in principle to younger children today. Scripture simply does not put a rod, or a paddle, in a parent's hands for childhood discipline. So we must go before God in faith and ask for insight. The Holy Spirit will guide us as God makes clear His desires for how we discipline our children in order to direct them to the Father.

✦

PART IV

PROTECTIVE

DISCIPLINE

CHAPTER 13

PROTECTING AGAINST
UNHEALTHY APPETITES

Discerning What Controls
Your Child's Desires

L ike all conscientious parents, Sally and I faced the dilemma of what to do about Saturday-morning cartoons. We indulged our children for a while with the few "innocent" cartoon series available when they were growing up, but it was clear that the reality of "betcha can't eat just one" was as true for children's television junk food as it was for potato chips. One show would be salted with previews for another creating a "just one more" mentality. The taste for one cartoon grew into an appetite for another, and the incessant and shameless marketing of cheap stuff and bad food resulted in unnecessary wants and desires in our children. Nothing feeds an appetite quite like watching television.

At some point we decided that cartoons didn't fit with what we wanted in our children's minds and hearts, and we declared an end to the cartoon era at the Clarkson home. Sally and I often resorted to "because" after trying in vain to explain why and from what we were trying to protect our children's hearts. Finally, Sally took out a piece of paper and drew a big, smiley-faced stick figure, replete with stick fingers and toes. Then she opened an art book and turned to an English painting from the 1800s of a boy in ruddy clothing with a welcoming smile. She held the two side by side and instructed her brood.

"The subject is the same in each of these drawings—it's a boy. Which of these is more interesting? Which do you want to know more about? Which would you want to spend time studying?" She stopped for dramatic effect, then continued. "If your dad and I say no to some things in your lives, it's not because we're mean; it's because we're good parents. We say no to the stick figures because we believe God has made your minds for the better things, like this beautiful, interesting painting. If we let you develop a taste for the crummy stuff and if that grew into a constant appetite for the mediocre, you might never develop an appetite for the excellent and beautiful things that reflect our Creator. We want to help you develop a taste and appetite for beauty and excellence."

We want to protect our children against mediocrity so that they can develop a healthy appetite for excellence and beauty. When it comes to protective discipline, I'm concerned about physical, emotional, and spiritual appetites—the personal desires we feed and develop. The word *appetite* comes from a compound of two Latin words that mean, literally, "to go to," but would be translated "strive after." An appetite is what we strive for and actively desire.

Why are appetites an issue of protective discipline? Simply put, whatever I allow my children to strive after is what will eventually fill their hearts and minds. Their appetites will define them. If I leave them to strive after things of the world that will never satisfy, those vain things will define them, leaving little hunger for better things. If I can minimize those appetites, however, and train my children to strive after excellence and beauty, those higher standards will define them. The adult adage "you are what you eat" has a different twist for children: "They will become what you let them eat." God has commissioned parents to direct the appetites that will define their children. In Ecclesiastes, we see the Preacher testing every earthly appetite in his pursuit of meaning, but he finds that "everything is futility and striving after wind" (Ecclesiastes 2:17). The material world apart from the life that God brings is nothing but vanity. Therefore, it's my responsibility as a parent to guide my children's appetites *away* from what is empty and *toward* desiring and finding the meaningful things of God.

APPETITES AND SIN

There is a deeper reason for training appetites, and that is to help children stand strong against sin. Most sin is not a crisis decision that suddenly happens. Instead we make small choices along the way that lead to bigger sin. It's like the dieter who sees a cake, takes a closer look, and "accidentally" gets some icing on his finger. He has to lick off the icing, which leads to having "just one little piece," and he winds up eating three big ones. Likewise, we ease our way into the big sins. Choices that seem innocent are really first steps in the direction of sin. If our children learn to recognize that pattern, they can train their appetites to resist lesser desires so that they can pursue the better ones.

We have within us a propensity to desire the lesser things. James explained in his first chapter that "each one is tempted when he is carried away and enticed by his own lust" (verse 14). We give in to our untrained desires and soon find ourselves on a slippery slope. "Then when lust has conceived, it gives birth to sin; and when sin is accomplished, it brings forth death" (verse 15). Once we indulge the desire, it's a steep slide into sin and spiritual death. And just to make sure his readers got the point, since the process is wrought with self-justification and rationalization, James threw in, "Do not be deceived, my beloved brethren" (verse 16).

Guard yourself from being deceived into thinking that childhood appetites are innocent, meaningless things. Though a child's appetites for "worldly things" may not lead her into any big sins as a child, the pattern of indulging childhood appetites for television programs, books, or activities can establish a pattern of worldly decisions that years later will lead to bigger sin. If our sons and daughters learn in childhood to follow their appetites without discernment, they will have to confront their bad habits as young adults and adults. So we parents need to start early helping our children learn discernment and self-denial, both of which are critical aspects of maturity. When we do so, we are protecting our children from patterns that would lead them away from God's blessing.

On the positive side, we are helping our children take steps in God's direction. Jesus said, "Blessed are those who hunger and thirst for righteousness, for they shall be satisfied" (Matthew 5:6). The happiest people are those whose appetite is set on knowing and doing what pleases God— they will be, literally, "filled up" with Him. Peter said, "like newborn babies, long for the pure milk of the word" (1 Peter 2:2). In other words, have the same natural, passionate appetite and desire for God's truth that a baby has for its mother's milk. Paul told the Colossians to "set your mind on the things above, not on the things that are on earth" (Colossians 3:2). The pursuit of godly things is a choice we make, for ourselves and for our children.

Here's the hard part: Your children will pick up their appetites for the things of God primarily from what *you* value, not just from what you want *them* to value. If you want them to desire the things that will lead them to God, then you will have to show them what that means. If you want your children to have an appetite for reading good books, they need to see you read good books. Your child has a natural appetite for knowledge and experience, but that appetite is undiscriminating when it comes to the difference between great and mediocre, ignoble and ennobling, worldly and godly. Too often, out of an unwillingness to take the time to provide something better, we satiate our children's appetites with childish, often worldly "food" that appeals to their immaturity rather than to their developing maturity. We see evidence of this when parents give in to their children's desires for a Playstation rather than encouraging them to learn a musical instrument or take up a new hobby. It also happens when parents surrender to the Saturday-morning cartoonfest rather than insisting that their children be creative with outdoor activities or the making of their own video movie. It happens when parents buy books that exist only to promote a movie or a character instead of books with quality writing and illustration. Sadly, we often fail to feed our children what they really need to be healthy and to grow strong in Christ.

DISCERNMENT FOR THE ENTIRE FAMILY

How can a parent discern between what is worldly and what is godly? So many things in a child's world have the appearance of acceptability, but beneath a thin veneer of respectability is the whisper, "Vanity of vanities! All is vanity" (Ecclesiastes 1:2). But exactly when does the childish become the worldly? Fortunately, God has provided a standard of measurement that can be applied to almost any situation. This equal-opportunity, all-ages standard works every time: "Finally, brethren, whatever is true, whatever is honorable, whatever is right, whatever is pure, whatever is lovely, whatever is of good repute, if there is any excellence and if anything worthy of praise, dwell on these things" (Philippians 4:8).

This admonition comes at the end of a series of thoughts about how to "stand firm in the Lord." After exhorting the Christians of Philippi to live in harmony, to rejoice in the Lord, to be patient, and to pray, Paul told them, quite literally, how to think. He knew that it's impossible to separate what you think from what you say and do ("For the mouth speaks out of that which fills the heart" [Matthew 12:34]). Paul didn't tell the Philippians exactly what to think (the rest of Scripture does that), but instead he gave them a grid by which to evaluate their thought life. It's a practical model for "taking every thought captive to the obedience of Christ" (2 Corinthians 10:5).

Paul recommended that we "dwell on these things" and provided eight mental filters for evaluating our thought life:

1. *Whatever is true...* Am I dwelling on things I know to be true about God and life instead of what I know to be false, deceitful, distorted, and unbiblical?

2. *Whatever is honorable...* Am I dwelling on things I know to be honoring to God and the things of God instead of what I know to be common, base, vulgar, and pagan?

3. *Whatever is right...* Am I dwelling on things I know conform to the ways and will of God instead of what I know to be ungodly, unrighteous, sinful, and wrong?

4. *Whatever is pure...* Am I dwelling on things I know to be holy and innocent instead of what I know to be dirty, lustful, impure, and unholy?

5. *Whatever is lovely...* Am I dwelling on things I know to be beautiful and inspiring instead of what I know to be ugly, degenerate, disgusting, and violent.

6. *Whatever is of good repute...* Am I dwelling on what I know to be acceptable to God instead of what I know to be disdainful, disreputable, cheap, and coarse?

7. *If there is any excellence...* Am I dwelling on what I know to be virtuous and worthy of the God who gave His excellent Son to redeem me instead of what I know to be worldly and mediocre?

8. *If anything worthy of praise...* Am I dwelling on what I know leads to the praise of God, instead of what I know to be of no eternal value?

Paul told the Philippians that they should "dwell on these things"—ponder and reflect on these things. But then, in the next verse, he added the exhortation to "practice these things." Whatever they had "learned and received and heard and seen" (Philippians 4:9) in him—all of the things he just mentioned—they were to put into practice. You and I and our children truly are what we think.

WHAT CONTROLS YOUR CHILD'S DESIRES?

Scripture is full of references to the "desires of your heart," but it speaks as much about the desires of the wicked as it does the desires of the righteous. We have control over our desires, and what we choose to desire shapes what we become. Understanding this, Jesus instructed us to "store up for yourselves treasures in heaven" rather than just "treasures on earth" because, He said, "where your treasure is, there your heart will be also" (Matthew 6:19-21). The appetite we choose to feed points our heart either to God or to the world.

How does this truth apply to protective discipline? No parent wants to be guilty of overkill by turning every issue into a spiritual decision. Some options truly are six of one, half-a-dozen of the other. But there are other arenas of appetite that will shape a child toward either faithfulness or unrighteousness (see Luke 16:10). So help your child take small steps of faithfulness now. Allow them the freedom to make small decisions about seemingly insignificant appetites. It will lead to greater faithfulness later. As you do this, you are practicing protective discipline that will keep your children from taking small steps toward unrighteousness that could lead to greater unrighteousness later.

Clearly it is important that we consider what occupies most of our children's time. As we do so, we will begin to see what they might value as they grow older. The following list will help you determine what controls your child's heart and what you want in your child's world. Vigilance in these areas has proved critical in shaping my own children's appetites and desires.

What Children Read

In the last twenty years or so, book publishing has exploded. Major bookstores have popped up everywhere, offering what seems like an endless supply of new books. Children's books have become a major market influence, and often adult-themed juvenile fiction leads the surge. Magazine racks have expanded from six feet of major magazines to forty feet or more of magazines covering every imaginable topic and interest. All of this means that children are awash in reading choices.

Stop for a moment, though, and consider the role of reading in God's eternal plan. The reason we enjoy reading books is because God designed us to learn from His Book. God determined that His eternal truth and His revelation of Himself would be preserved in written form for all eternity. He preserved His Word in sacred writings. The Lamb's Book of Life (not the Lamb's Web-enabled DVD of life) is a real, physical book with the names of God's elect written in it. The gospel of John was written so that readers would "believe that Jesus is the Christ" (John 20:31).

As the tidal wave of books and magazines (we won't talk about catalogs, cereal boxes, and junk mail!) has washed over us, it's not hard to see the effects on the lives of our children. Reading materials that appeal to earthly and worldly desires comprise a growing segment of the publishing boom. If one of Satan's strategies is to distract us from the written Word of God by flooding our lives with inferior reading choices, then he seems to be succeeding.

All of these reading choices call for protective discipline. I don't suggest that we crack down on legitimate areas of interest, ability, or skill, but rather on materials that are vain pursuits of information or things and a waste of time, mental energy, and heart devotion. This will be a judgment call for every family, but that's what discernment means. For instance, if you have a child interested in computers, you wouldn't discourage a book on the history of the personal computer or a magazine devoted to computer issues. However, you might actively discourage computer game magazines or books on mastering a particular computer game.

On the positive side, we can try to balance things out by cultivating our children's appetites for the very best literature. Sally and I have read good books—storybooks, children's literature, historical stories, illustrated topical books, and many others—aloud from the beginning of our children's lives. Hearing good books and literature read by their parents makes clear to children what their parents' values are, so it's a natural step for children to want to read on their own books like the ones their parents have read to them.

Sally and I have also been discriminating in the kinds of books we acquire and keep at home. Gladys Hunt in her classic book on books, *Honey for a Child's Heart,* reminds parents, "Good books have genuine spiritual substance, not just intellectual enjoyment. Books help children know what to look for in life. Reading develops the taste buds of the mind as children learn to savor what is seen, heard, and experienced and fit these into some kind of worthwhile framework."[1] Unfortunately, the explosion in children's publishing has meant that what some would call "twaddle"— shallow, vain, dull, pedantic books for children—has also increased exponentially. Even the Christian publishing industry pours out twaddle. (Just because it's "Christian" doesn't make it worthy reading material.) It takes constant vigilance and effort to recommend and promote the best reading choices for our children and to minimize the temptation they face to be drawn away by twaddle. A home library of twaddle-free books is one of the best lines of defense.

What Children Watch

Perhaps the most dangerous appetite is for television and videos, not because the medium is inherently evil, but because the act of watching wastes copious amounts of their time and mental energies. Television is, by nature, a time- and attention-intensive medium because it requires passive consumption by your child for extended periods. Rather than truly engaging your child's imagination, television replaces imaginative creativity with inactive sensory engagement, which actually has a dulling effect on mental faculties. Reading, in contrast, requires active mental effort and active visual and mental engagement—all of which feed the imagination. Video requires neither. More than that, though, time spent passively taking in video output means that much less time is available for reading good books, the one appetite that holds the most potential for impacting your child's heart and mind for God.

That's not to say there aren't many excellent television programs that are mentally and spiritually uplifting, and we enjoy those as a family. However, we also realize that video viewing comes with a price: The act of watching reinforces an appetite for the medium itself. There is an addictive quality to the passivity of television. Therefore, our strategy as parents is not about how to get the most out of television and video watching, but how to lessen its negative impact and time consumption, so that our children have more time to develop appetites for reading and the things of real life. We'll take a closer look at television content in chapter 15.

What Children Listen To

For most families, mine included, music is a natural part of everything we do. We listen to it, sing along with it, study it, write it, and perform it. We do have discriminating tastes, though, and are sensitive to what kinds of music we "feed" our younger children. (By the time they are teens, we trust them to feed themselves.) We are not a "hymns and classical only" family, although we greatly enjoy both. We recognize and also enjoy a wide range of styles and genres that fit the Philippians 4 grid, music ranging from classical to acoustic instrumental, folk to country, gospel to contemporary Christian, show tunes to cowboy, piano to hammered dulcimer, and many others. In all of them, though, we tenaciously hold to high standards of goodness and excellence in composition, performance, and production. We watch our appetites.

Rather than taking the negative "that's not good music" approach, though, we try hard to shape our children's musical tastes and appetites with a positive "that's good music!" approach. By consistently exposing them to quality musical choices, we train their appetites toward excellence. In that process, though, we are ruthless in rejecting music that rejects God.

We are also quick to determine whether the musical style appeals more to the natural or fleshly side of our nature (with overemphasized beat and rhythm, excessive noise, grating vocals or instrumentals) or to the spiritual side (emphasizing melody, harmony, supporting but not dominant rhythm, and appealing vocals and instrumentals). The bottom line is being diligent to protect our children from musical appetites that could lead them away from God.

Music is a defining force for children because musical styles represent cultural values. The kind of music your child learns to desire can, over time, shape how she thinks about life and the world. In a demographically defined culture such as ours, every musical style is marketed to a segment of society, so you can be defined to some degree by the music you choose to consume. Musical appetites created in childhood can play a major role in defining your child's values and perspectives on life as he or she grows up.

What Children Are Amused By

We want our children to be able to find their own sources of amusement so that they can entertain themselves. Children who are more introverted do this naturally, while extroverted children need some help, but all children need to be able to fill up their own hours. However, not all amusements are profitable. In fact, one respected dictionary describes the history of the word *amuse* as derived from a term that means "to stare stupidly," with a secondary meaning "to delude or deceive."[2] This is not the kind of amusement I have in mind, although television seems to fit the definition. How your child fills up his mind when left to his own devices will have a profound impact on his appetites.

Imaginative play is a good example. We decided when our children were young that we wouldn't allow them to pretend things that God would condemn in real life. I wanted our boys to pretend they were brave and honorable war heroes, but I was careful to discourage them from pretending to kill others, even the enemy, with callous disregard. Toughness was encouraged, but they weren't allowed to pretend murder, wanton violence, or cruelty either in their actions or words. Similarly, when pretending to be a mother, our girls weren't allowed to treat their dolls roughly or unkindly, but rather were encouraged to offer their babies tenderness and affection. We also discouraged our children from pretending to be sensual or worldly, or even violent or rough, in a way that negated scriptural teaching to have "a gentle and quiet spirit, which is precious in the sight of God" (1 Peter 3:4).

Toys and games can also encourage an ungodly imagination. Many of the action figures that are so popular with boys raised in a generation saturated in fantasy are not merely caricatures, but distortions of humanity. They don't look like real people, and they encourage a kind of fantasy play that is detached from real life. While many figures that represented real people were fun for our boys, we chose not to allow our children to pretend with figures that looked demonic, otherworldly, or ungodly. These were not the images we wanted populating our children's imaginations. In the same way, we were careful to avoid games based on ungodly fantasy themes, unbiblical supernatural themes, or worldly themes such as greed, conquest, sexuality, or dishonesty. Instead we looked for toys and games that passed the Philippians 4:8 test and created appetites that were consistent with biblical teaching and godly living.

The computer is fast becoming the dominant form of personal amusement for children. Because using a computer is a multisensory experience, the kinds of computer amusements and games you allow your children to consume will have a lasting influence on their appetites in other areas. The bar that separates what is appropriate for children or adults is always being pushed lower, and more and more adult themes are creeping into children's programs. While we can determine what programs we will buy for our children, the Internet is another matter altogether. It's much more difficult to control, which makes the need for controls all the more necessary. As an appetite, it can become an overpowering desire, and for some children it can become almost addictive. So it's critical that parents carefully control how their children access and use the Internet. Despite all the benefits of the World Wide Web, we need to control our child's appetite for surfing the Net, and even for how they use e-mail. Computer appetites can quickly overtake all others.

TRAINING APPETITES ALONG THE PATH OF LIFE

Human appetites are so wide ranging that we could spend many more pages discussing art, activities, sports, hobbies, and many more categories. The few mentioned above, though, will give you a way to start thinking about how to apply the standard of Philippians 4:8 to your children's appetites. As you walk along the path of life with your children, you exercise protective discipline by helping them discern what their hearts and minds should hunger for. With your arm of protection, you keep them from being drawn away by desires that could lead them off the path and away from God. This training requires constant interaction and relationship. One look at the millions of prodigals and rudderless children around us today should convince you to take your child's appetites seriously. The right ones lead to life; the wrong ones, to suffering and death.

Jesus said, "Seek first His kingdom and His righteousness, and all these things will be added to you" (Matthew 6:33). All of us, our children included, have drives, desires, and goals we want to strive after. The biblical response to all of these appetites is to *seek first* God's kingdom and His path of righteousness. When those are the appetites that drive a life, everything else will fall into place.

CHAPTER 14

PROTECTING AGAINST HARMFUL RELATIONSHIPS

Discerning Who Holds Your Child's Heart

C hildren naturally want to do what their friends do. I've seen my children imitate the language, mannerisms, likes, dislikes, and even personality traits of other kids. In the teen years, we see it as "peer dependency" or "peer pressure," and we try to mitigate it. In childhood, though, we just think it's cute and see nothing that warrants concern. After all, they're just children. They'll grow out of it.

In reality, just the opposite is true. Children grow *into* it. Relational patterns established in childhood rarely just disappear in young adulthood. Consider Eli, the high priest in the Old Testament. His sons were teenagers *(naar)* who didn't know God, who sinned without shame, and who refused to honor their father (see 1 Samuel 3:12-17). It's clear that Eli didn't train them well when they were children and that he also failed to correct them as young men. Remember, too, the parable of the sower: If your children are to be inclined to trust God and grow in Him, the soil of their hearts must first be carefully cultivated.

In past eras, parents and the family were the primary gardeners who cultivated a child's heart. Today that influence is shared or, more accurately, *overshadowed,* by the influence of age-mates and teachers in a pervasive educational system. The "all the time and every place" influence of family in God's original design (see Deuteronomy 6:4-9) has been turned on its head in a culture that leaves almost no time and no place for parents, much less the family unit, to influence children. Our culture pushes parents to raise children who excel academically, athletically, musically, socially, and every other way. School and extracurricular activities fill a child's life, minimizing family time and influence. This radical shift in influence has been generated by societal conditions, including higher mobility, two-income families, and government funding of education and other child-related programs.

The most commonly stated justification for this radical turnaround of priorities is *socialization,* a term coined by social scientists in the twentieth century and influenced by socialist ideology. The goal of socialization is to promote the public education of all children. Its basic premise is that a child needs extensive contact with age-mates in order to conform and adapt to the group so she can function well within society. Not long ago in a television interview, one evolutionist professor argued, quite seriously, that the parents' role in human development is irrelevant because children and teens will choose to adapt to their own group. As nonsensical as that sounds, it's the ultimate expression of socialization in a secular society.

While most Christian parents would reject that idea as extreme, they nonetheless believe that their children need the experience of socialization. They have accepted the secular notion that the family alone is not enough to "socialize" young children. However, if asked for a biblical perspective on the insufficiency of the family, they would be hard-pressed to provide one.

Contrast this with a plain teaching from Scripture. In one of Paul's most precise statements about our relationship to culture, we are commanded, "Do not be conformed to this world, but be transformed by the renewing of your mind, so that you may prove what the will of God is, that which is good and acceptable and perfect" (Romans 12:2). God calls us to stop letting the current age's thought patterns shape our thinking. Instead, our thinking must be transformed by God's truth, which is true for every culture in every time. Likewise, if our children find it easy to conform to the ways and values of their age-mates, who many times are disconnected from the transforming power of God's Word, then we need to ask whether we are providing the protective discipline they need.

Some Christians suggest that being exposed to a secular environment is a good thing for young children so that they can learn to be salt and light in their world. Parents' concern that their children be witnesses for Christ overrides their concerns about their children's exposure to negative influences. However, Scripture places the responsibility to witness for Christ only on young adults and adults who have more fully developed moral and spiritual capacities, which enable them to resist the culture's conforming influences. Children are not expected in Scripture either to be evangelists or missionaries, or to exercise spiritual discernment that they do not yet possess. Rather, childhood is viewed as a time during which children are guided and protected by parents who are preparing them to be faithful. Social and cultural changes, not biblical ideals, have taken children away from that family environment during the vulnerable years of childhood and thrust them prematurely into social settings. Even in the case of a confident child who wants to tell his friends about Jesus, his parents would be wise to recognize their son's vulnerability. Until your children reach young adulthood and develop spiritual discernment that will lead to maturity, they are just as likely to be pulled down by other children as they are to pull the other children up.

Clearly, we need to be aware of secular philosophies regarding the socialization of children so we'll be better able to exercise protective discipline in the area of relationships. A big part of heartfelt discipline involves first recognizing the need for much more parental influence than our culture encourages and then making adjustments in family lifestyle to recover some of our rightful influence. It doesn't take a government-funded study to reach the commonsense conclusion that peer influence rises and parental influence falls when children spend a great part of their week in the company of other children their age. Your children's God-given needs for relational attachment to their parents will be diluted by the attachments they form with other children. If you don't make a concerted effort to cultivate and maintain their attachment to you when they are with you, they will begin to look elsewhere to meet that need. The quality of your relationship with your children during the school years will set the pattern for your relationship with them as young adults as well as for the kind of people they will become.

As we saw in chapter 2, in God's design parents and the family are to be the primary influences in a child's life.[1] But we have drifted far from that biblical ideal. Where once the family was the center of a child's social and intellectual preadolescent development, now school has taken over much of that role. Where once the family was the center of a child's spiritual development, now churches have become surrogate parents. Where once the family was the center of a child's recreational life, now media, sports, and other activities keep children entertained and amused.

In a culture where mothers are no longer encouraged to stay home with their children and fathers are often disengaged from home life, it's not hard to understand why the family is fragmenting. As parents abandon the home front, whether by choice or necessity, it is only natural for social institutions to step in to fill the void. And without a strong biblical base guiding those social institutions, how can we deny the increased possibility of negative influence on our children?

"Because a child's companionships are so influential, it is [all] the more important that they be closely watched and carefully guided by the child's parents," wrote H. Clay Trumbull, a leader in the American Sunday school movement in the late 1800s. "It is a parent's duty to know who are his child's companions, and to know the character, and course of conduct, and influence upon his child, of every one of those companions separately.... Knowing his child's companionships, a parent ought to encourage such of them as are worthiest, and discourage such as he cannot approve.... To neglect this agency of a child's training, would be to endanger his entire career in life, whatever else were done in his behalf."[2] That advice was written at a time when family influence was still strong and the schools were still a servant in instilling Christian values and character rather than a master of secular socialization, as they are today.

In the area of relationships and companions, perhaps more than any other area of protective discipline, you need to be guarding your child's heart because children are not yet able to do that for themselves. You are providing discernment in relationships that they are not yet able to exercise on their own. One unsupervised relationship could impact your child for the rest of her life. And I don't mean only a friend's bad character that your child might emulate, but other dangerous influences such as exposure to undesirable media, introduction to sexual information, the influence of another child's ungodly parents, and much more.

RELATIONSHIPS AND PROTECTIVE DISCIPLINE

There are really two aspects to protective discipline in the area of relationships: a strong defense and a confident offense. On the defensive front, you need to guard your child against four kinds of dangerous relationships: fools, unbelievers, immoral people, and false teachers.

Fools

"He who walks with wise men will be wise, but the companion of fools will suffer harm" (Proverbs 13:20). The companions that you allow into your child's life, even at an early age, will lead either to wisdom or to harm. Parents are the companions from whom children should glean the most wisdom (see Deuteronomy 6:4-9; Ephesians 6:4). Though Proverbs 13:20 is probably directed to young adults, the principle holds true for children, too. Young friends, although not "fools" in the Proverbs sense of the word, can nonetheless influence other children in foolishness. So even young children need a parent to wisely and lovingly supervise and guide their inter-actions and companionships.

Being mostly in the company of other children for much of the day puts children at risk of being attracted to and tempted by foolish choices. They are also harmed to the degree that they don't have a wise adult watch-ing over them. I still carry the memories of images and ideas to which I was exposed by childhood friends at school and in the neighborhood. Those harmful images and ideas temporarily led me in destructive paths, and they never completely go away—which is why it's so critical to protect your child against the wrong kinds of relationships.

An even greater harm can befall your child if you leave him under the supervision of a foolish adult. In a day of rampant sexual abuse, that dan-ger obviously comes to mind, but there are many other ways a foolish adult can harm a child, from exposure to undesirable words and ideas to physi-cal danger due to that adult's irresponsibility. This guideline applies even to grandparents, aunts, uncles, and other relatives who are not wise.

Unbelievers

Sally and I have always allowed our kids to play with both believing and unbelieving children as long as we were able to supervise their interactions. However, we learned early on that the biblical principle of the yoke can be applied to our children as well as to us as adults. Paul told the Corinthian Christians, "Do not be bound together with unbelievers; for what partner-ship have righteousness and lawlessness, or what fellowship has light with darkness? Or what harmony has Christ with Belial, or what has a believer in common with an unbeliever?" (2 Corinthians 6:14-15). We saw an application of this principle worked out in our daughter Sarah's life. She became friends with an unbelieving girl, and they were soon spending a lot of time together. I noticed that a bond was growing that created a mixing of desires, values, and influences. Although the grown-up version of a yoke is a mutual bonding by agreement in marriage or business, the childish version can be an emotional bonding in friendship, the allegiance of two immature hearts, a believing child and a nonbelieving child. Although Sarah and the other girl remained friends and Sarah also tried to be a witness for Christ, we created some distance between them in order to discourage the immature emotional bonding. In place of this relationship, we sought out other good and godly friends for our daughter.

Your protective discipline in your child's life should help him avoid becoming unequally yoked emotionally as well as spiritually. You may have to encourage your child to wait and pray, to trust God to provide a believing friend. Far from being harmed by the experience, your child will grow spiritually in the process of waiting.

Immoral People

It may seem evident that you should protect your children from the influences of immoral people, but because of the open nature of American culture, doing so is not that easy. Our culture is immoral, and our children see it through media and the lifestyles around them. Issues of immorality—such as drug abuse, violence, homosexuality, prostitution, teen pregnancy, and others—which once were discussed only discreetly are now headline news and are sometimes even celebrated and promoted. So even if you are able to constrain the impact of immorality on your children at home, they are certainly hearing from friends or acquaintances much more than you want them to know.

When Sally and I think about our own growing-up years, we realize that everything immoral that impacted our lives was experienced at school or in school relationships. With children exposed to more and more indecency and immorality through media, the Internet, and even in the classroom, this issue of protection isn't just about teenagers anymore. Even young friends can expose your child to immoral language, attitudes, and behaviors that you may never know about.

False Teachers

It's possible for very nice people to hold very wrong views about truth, God, Jesus, and life. When these views are presented in an appealing way, we need spiritual discernment to identify the errors. But children can't easily discern between false teaching and truth, whether the teaching involves nuances of meaning or blatant falsehood. When the teaching is coming from someone you have approved of by placing your child under that person's authority, it is even more difficult for your child to know whom or what to believe. Parents must both discern whether a person might be a false teacher and protect their children from the confusion that a person's teaching could generate.

Taking the Offensive

Given the nature of schools, it's difficult if not impossible to protect your child from all relationships that might be harmful. But the other side of the relationship issue—going on the offensive by building a good relationship with your children and becoming the primary influence in their lives—is perhaps even more important. I'm talking about reclaiming your biblical role as a parent in the life of your child and reestablishing the family as central to your child's life. Here are some ways you can go on the offensive.

Spend More Time with Your Children

The cords of emotional attachment between you and your child's heart are strengthened by spending meaningful time together. It's not just quality time that builds bonds between your hearts, but quantity time (remember the "all the time and every place" model in Deuteronomy?). Quality is important because it needs to be meaningful time: Reading a story together is quality time; watching a cartoon is not. But quantity is important for the simple reason that it takes time to build and maintain a relationship of trust and love, especially when so many other things compete for that time. In his book *The Child Influencers,* Dan Adams says, "Many of the things we commit our time to are very good, but if you are *over-committed* to anything else, you are *under-committed* to your family."[3]

There is a limitless range of ways you can reclaim relational time with your children. Having family devotionals and family nights will create a good foundation, but deep relational bonds are built by sharing a variety of experiences. Make time to take your children on dates for ice cream and conversation. Take a few minutes at bedtime to talk to your child and pray about what's on her mind. Start reading a book aloud together and talking about it. Plan some active family outings, such as hiking, going on a picnic, visiting a park or the zoo (and put these activities on your calendar). Make it a point to talk about schoolwork and what is happening at school. Get involved in a community outreach or service together.

And keep in mind that, when you're not available, your children will seek to have their relational and emotional needs filled by others. Dr. Ross Campbell, author of *Relational Parenting,* emphasizes in his book that one of the primary roles parents play is to keep their child's "emotional tank" (his metaphor for a child's emotional needs) filled up through unconditional love and gentle discipline. He admits that it takes time to do that: "Yes, giving focused attention is often time-consuming and can seem burdensome to already exhausted parents. But it is the most powerful means you have in keeping your children's emotional tanks full and investing in their future."[4] He suggests many strategies for being the one who fills your child's emotional tank, but it happens primarily when you give your children the one-on-one, personal attention they need and are designed to want from you. And that means making time in your life for them.

Make Your Home Inviting, Warm, and Safe

Before we had our first child, Sally and I had decided that we would do everything we could to make sure our home was, in our children's minds, the warmest, safest, most enjoyable home they would know. Doing so would be a positive means of protective discipline that would keep them close to us. If they were drawn to the toys and privileges of a friend's home, that would be a warning to us—not a warning that we needed to give them more cultural stuff, but that we needed to give them more love. We believed then—and we believe even more strongly today, now that our children are older—that in some way their love for our home would be a barometer of our love for them. If they felt loved and accepted in our home, our reasoning went, they would prefer being here than anywhere else. So we work hard to keep the atmosphere of our home loving and warm.

We also work hard to make the home environment interesting and stimulating. Rather than filling our home with time-wasting media and mind-numbing video games, we fill our home with hundreds of fascinating books, a variety of musical instruments, hands-on creative crafts and resources, thoughtful interactive games, excellent music and videos, and various fun things to do. We make sure our children have hobbies and interests that they can pursue and appreciate at home. We also make a concerted effort to do things together at home whenever we can—games, movie nights, music, and more.

As a result, it's usually our home that neighborhood children prefer, mostly because our children prefer being in our home. In a way, we are practicing hospitality (see Romans 12:13) not just for others who may come to our home, but for our own children, too. We make them feel welcomed and special by working to make our home the place they want to be. The greatest benefit of our efforts has been the protective discipline it has provided because they want to be home with us.

Create a Safety Net of Relationships

If there were a biblical concept of socialization, it would probably be Proverbs 13:20, which reminds us that "He who walks with wise men will be wise." Wisdom is acquired by being around wise people. The biblical concept of *koinonia,* or fellowship, is the New Testament equivalent of walking with the wise. We share a life "in common" with one another, what we call the community of believers. One of the purposes of that community is "to stimulate one another to love and good deeds" (Hebrews 10:24). The New Testament affirms the family as the primary influence in a child's life,[5] but your children also need to see the body of Christ loving and helping one another, bearing one another's burdens, and serving one another. The real value of the church for children is not the children's education program and activities, but the exposure to other families like yours. Your kids need to be around other intact families that are committed to their children just as you are to yours. They need to build relational bridges to believers of all different ages, not just their own family members.

To create and sustain this safety net of relationships, plan how you can get to know and spend time with like-minded families at church. Seek out relationships with families that share your values and beliefs as well as your commitment to your children. Your goal is not just to find another social activity to plug into your week, but to find a family relationship that will reinforce your own efforts to lead your children onto and along God's path of life. You might also consider finding or starting a small-group ministry in which whole families participate together in fellowship and Bible study. We recently started a midweek family class in our church in which the fellowship and instruction are directed to entire family units. Fathers take turns leading the class so children can see that other dads also teach the Scriptures to their children.

Know Your Child's Friends and the Friends' Families

Long ago, Sally and I established a family policy that we wouldn't let our children play at another child's house until we had met both the child and his or her parents. The idea of "innocent" child's play has been shoved off the road in our fast-moving culture, so we want to know what kinds of things our children will be exposed to. Many times we have the friend play at our house first so we can monitor the playtime and hear what's on that child's heart. Before our child can play at another child's house, though, we visit with the parents. We've had very pleasant children come over, but then we learn what kinds of television shows and movies are watched and what kinds of video games are played at that child's house. We might conclude that we need to be a Christian witness to that family, but having our child play there would not be part of our outreach strategy. Our responsibility is to protect our child from a relationship that could lead to harm.

DISCERNING WHO HOLDS YOUR CHILD'S HEART

Psalm 1 begins with a description of the "blessed man" as one "who does not walk in the counsel of the wicked, nor stand in the path of sinners, nor sit in the seat of scoffers" (Psalm 1:1). The psalmist could just as easily have said that the blessed person is the individual who is not wicked, who turns from sin, and who is not a scoffer. It is significant, though, that he casts the blessings of God in a relational mold: The blessing comes from *rejecting* foolish and unwise *relationships*. Paul affirmed that principle when he quoted a Greek play to admonish the Corinthian believers, "Do not be deceived: 'Bad company corrupts good morals'" (1 Corinthians 15:33). God knows that many sinful thoughts, attitudes, and habits are contracted through association with others. When you exercise protective discipline over your children in the area of relationships, you are simply trying to keep them from catching the sins of others. Stated positively, you are putting your children on God's path to greatest blessing by keeping them from walking in the wrong direction.

As you exercise protective discipline, don't stop with merely guarding against negative relationships. Rather, bring alive the truth for your children that "he who walks with wise men will become wise." Take the offensive to make this wisdom real for your children. By God's grace, you are creating cords of attachment between you and your child's heart. If your relationship with your children is strong and growing, it will provide a protective covering as they navigate relationships at school, in the neighborhood, and at church. God has designed your children's hearts to find their emotional grounding in you. If they do, your children will look less to those outside the family to fill the emotional tank in their hearts. They'll find all they need at home.

PROTECTING AGAINST
UNHEALTHY MEDIA

Discerning What Captures
Your Child's Imagination

W e're all buried under too much information, and we're hassled by too many competing messages. But even as the tide of the information age rises, we're actually still at low tide. More than a decade ago, I heard a speaker describing the number of discrete, targeted messages we receive each day. At the turn of the twentieth century it was about three hundred messages. By midcentury, it was a few thousand. In the late 1980s, it was twenty thousand and rising. Fifteen years later, the number has risen steadily and shows no signs of slowing. We haven't begun to see the amount of information that one planet can hold.

The messages of truth, the ideas and ideals of Christianity, are harder to hear in a world drowning in this sensory overload. In his book *A Landscape with Dragons,* Michael O'Brien writes, "In the entire history of mankind there has never been such a continuous bombardment of the human brain. The ever-present background throb of machinery, the roar of traffic, the high-pitched buzz of fluorescent lights, Muzak in elevators and supermarkets, herds of joggers wearing walkmans, a gaggle of talkshows. A world drowning in chatter!"[1] Consider that a child has not yet developed mental filters to tune out the useless noise—that fact means it's all going in. The messages of God's truth can easily become just part of the cacophony of life. "We can gradually come to think that the torrent of noise is normal," says O'Brien, and "when the pressures become intolerable we might even begin to agree with what the noise is saying."[2]

More than ever children are exposed to and endangered by information that is inappropriate and even harmful, and all too easily accessed. That threat is heightened by the growth of visual media to communicate messages that can quickly capture a child's attention and imagination. Few messages coming from the secular world are consistent with Christian belief and practice. And as digital technology continues to evolve, children will be most vulnerable to those messages.

One thing is patently obvious: Media are the delivery systems for nearly all forms of information. By media, I mean television, radio, the Internet, newspapers, magazines, CDs, DVDs, and others that are either emerging or yet to be invented. So while your children will want to know how to use the media to their advantage, you must ensure that the media don't take advantage of your children while they are young, competing with God's purpose that you be their primary source of information about the world and about life.

FROM THE IMAGINATION INTO THE HEART

Without merely condemning media, we need to consider the impact of media content on our children's imaginations because what captures their imagination will feed their hearts. The imagination conceives of things that may or may not exist in the physical world. If your children's imaginations feed on information and images that are consistent with Christian truth, they will be able to imagine spiritual realities, things that require the eyes of the heart to see. If your child's imagination is shaped by non-Christian thoughts and images, especially media images of a supernatural or other-worldly nature, those will create a conflict in your child's heart. Michael

O'Brien warns: "We would be sadly mistaken if we assumed that the cultural revolution is mainly a conflict of ideas. It is primarily spiritual warfare.… The invasion reaches into very young minds, attempting to implant there at the earliest possible moment an exaltation of the diabolical."[3] Even a cursory glance at children's programming finds "good" witches, heroes with no moral anchors, superheroes with demonic-like appearances and power, children with supernatural powers that don't come from God, false gods, pagan and humanistic themes, and much more.

There is no question that the media have introduced both great evil and great good to our world. In exercising protective discipline in your child's life, though, the issue must be more than simply finding a balance between the two. Rather, our task is to minimize the evil influence and maximize the good. In our market-driven economy, owners of information and entertainment resort to whatever will capture your attention—or your child's—in order to elicit a response. So the ocean of information that washes over us is not neutral. It has an agenda behind it, and your children are standing right in its path. If your children have ever sung an advertising jingle they heard only once, or wanted a pet, a toy, or an electronic gizmo they saw in a movie or television show, you know they are vulnerable. As the tide of information rises, one way you protect your children is by making sure they know not only how to swim safely and wisely in this ocean, but also when to get out of the water.

Paul admonished the Ephesian believers, "Do not participate in the unfruitful deeds of darkness, but instead even expose them; for it is disgraceful even to speak of the things which are done by them in secret" (5:11-12). He challenged Christians to show by the quality of their lives that they are children of light—to be characterized by "goodness and righteousness and truth, trying to learn what is pleasing to the Lord" (5:9-10). Simply by *being* light their lives will expose the darkness. They don't have to mention the disgraceful details of what happens in the darkness because the light of their own lives will expose it.

Long before the advent of mass media, King David voiced the same principles in Psalm 101. He told God he would "give heed to the blameless way" and that he would "walk within my house in the integrity of my heart" (verse 2). For us as parents, integrity of the heart is closely related to our protective discipline. Children need to know that there is light and there is darkness. As we protect our children from the darkness, we also must ourselves refuse to "participate in the unfruitful deeds of darkness" (Ephesians 5:11). We can't tell our children it's harmful for them and then live as though it does no harm in our own lives. David said, "I will set no worthless thing before my eyes" (Psalm 101:3). Some have called this principle God's *TV Guide*. Children are smart enough to recognize when their parents consume worthless media content. When that parent tells a child she can't watch a certain Saturday-morning cartoon, the child knows the parent doesn't *really* think television is harmful. This may be a small thing in a parent's eyes, but it's a big thing to a child.

David said, "I hate the work of those who fall away.... A perverse heart shall depart from me; I will know no evil" (Psalm 101:3-4). I cannot agree with David's words in a family devotional in the morning, but then turn around that evening and welcome perverse and evil men into my home when I flip on the television. My children need to see me hate the same sinful things that I am protecting them from. It's an issue of integrity. I want to say with David, "My eyes shall be upon the faithful of the land, that they may dwell with me; he who walks in a blameless way is the one who will minister to me" (Psalm 101:6).

My goal is not to teach my children to condemn everything that is wrong, but rather to have them be known by their Christian character and conduct when it comes to the use of the media. My children's light will not shine brighter because they know the darkness, but because they know the Light. Paul challenged the Philippian believers to "prove yourselves to be blameless and innocent, children of God above reproach in the midst of a crooked and perverse generation, among whom you appear as lights in the world, holding fast the word of life" (2:15-16). The reason Christians should live up to that challenge, Paul said, is because of the light within them: "For it is God who is at work in you, both to will and to work for His good pleasure" (verse 13). Protective discipline demands that we do all we can to make sure that the light shines brightly in our children as they prepare to hold fast the Word of Life in their own crooked and perverse generation.

DARKNESS VERSUS LIGHT

The dark side of the media wants to steal your child's imagination and convert it to worldly and non-Christian views. In the Harry Potter books and feature-length films, children learn about occult practices, sorcery, and incantations that once were cloaked from children's view but now are presented as entertainment. In Saturday-morning cartoons, children are regularly exposed to New Age and spiritualist practices such as crystal power, channeling, reincarnation, spiritism, and more. In after-school programming, children hear and see humanistic and self-centered philosophies of life and sexuality.

During your child's vulnerable years, you must exercise your strongest protective discipline. The content of today's mass media is part of a large-scale spiritual battle for the mind, imagination, and heart of your child. God expects you to "take up the full armor of God, so that you will be able to resist in the evil day, and having done everything, to stand firm" (Ephesians 6:13). Your child, like a young page serving a knight, is not yet ready to wear the "full armor," so you must be his protector. Your child is learning from you until he is ready to wear the armor on his own.

There are also prevalent themes ("schemes"?) that run through much of the media's dark side. If these themes are not part of a larger conspiracy to corrupt children's minds, they are at the very least expressions of a corrupt industry conspiring to make as much money as possible. Either way, we must exercise protective discipline to guard our children's vulnerable imaginations. The themes that should concern us most include the occult, the supernatural, science fiction, graphic violence, casual sexuality, dysfunctional lifestyles, and coarse language. Let's look at each one briefly.

The Occult

As North American culture has drifted further from Christian values and understandings, few Christians should be surprised that occult themes have entered society's mainstream. What is surprising, though, is the vast popularity of occultism among the broad population and the horrific ways it is depicted. And with Harry Potter leading the charge, it's a commercially exploited children's marketing theme promising to create a generation of spin-offs that will keep children feeding on the occult for years to come.

To allow your child's imagination to be filled with the images and stories of evil and wickedness, especially those depicted in adult-oriented "entertainment," would be tantamount to dropping your sword, stepping aside, and telling Satan, "Go ahead. Take your best shot." But what about the milder portrayals seen in children's books in the form of characters who only dabble with spells and other supernatural phenomena? The danger here is the trivialization of that which God says is condemnable.[4] Your child should learn that no form of the occult is trivial, and neither is it entertaining. When you keep the occult out of your home, no matter how "innocently" and entertainingly it may be presented, you will protect your child's vulnerable spirit from the subtle attacks of Satan.

The Supernatural

In news and entertainment programs alike, the major media love to explore supernatural themes. In print and on the screen, media outlets proffer views of what God is like and stir a stewpot of beliefs, theories, and experiences that support nearly every view of God, mankind, and the afterlife. With only a few rare exceptions, noticeably absent from the discussion is an orthodox view of Christianity. Some of the most popular movies in recent years for both children and older audiences have included supernatural themes dealing with ghosts, the spirit world, demons, angels (the secular kind), and more. The supernatural is a common theme in programming targeted to children.

Parents should proceed cautiously when this theme pops up. There is much in the way of good family programming that contains a kind of benign and benevolent God. However, there is very little in children's programming that doesn't turn the supernatural into a "making God in my own image" program. Supernatural fantasy themes are just part of the noise of our culture that competes with the Bible's real supernatural truth. Though most children could distinguish between supernatural fantasy and biblical truth, why should they have to? It's a waste of a Christian's imagination.

Science Fiction

Science fiction is as much a part of modern childhood culture as John Wayne westerns were a part of the previous generation's experience. The semireal world of cowboys and Indians just kind of segued into intergalactic battles and space aliens. Children's imaginations have made a giant shift from the "real world" stories of the American West to the fantasy-world stories of realms unknown to physical reality. Science fiction may seem fun and frivolous at first glance, but its fantasy world is anything but morally neutral. In reality, it is not "science fiction" but "science fantasy," and it is guided by a worldview that contains no God, no original sin, and no Savior. The world of science fantasy is populated by aliens, creatures, and beings that counterfeit divine power but usually claim to have evolved beyond the primitive need for religion. Even when there is a "god" in the picture, it's a false god.

Because science fiction led me away from God as a child, I am perhaps more sensitive to it than other Christians might be. It's not the genre alone that concerns me, since our family has enjoyed writers such as C. S. Lewis and J. R. R. Tolkien, and I certainly enjoy good science fiction writing. However, there is no harm in delaying or restricting your children's exposure to science fiction. I delayed letting our boys watch the Star Wars trilogy until Nathan was about twelve years old. Then we watched it together and had a great discussion about the movies. I believe that this timing prevented my sons from being drawn too early into a fascination with the fantasy world of contemporary science fiction.

I know from experience that the competing views of life and God found in science fiction can become a stumbling block to faith for a child who is not yet able to sort out fiction, fantasy, and faith. Stories of "intelligent" life on other planets, UFOs, and aliens can become actual possibilities in the mind of a child, leading to doubt, fear, or obsession in some children—feelings they might not share with a parent. The commercialization of science fiction makes it seem acceptable to children, but it's merely a marketing veneer that covers the genre's underlying assumptions. It's okay for kids to wait until they are old enough to appreciate fantasy for what it is and not confuse it with reality. You can be the judge of when your child is able to distinguish between the two.

Graphic Violence

There is no justification for exposing a child to any depiction of graphic violence. Many of today's most popular computer and video games involve characters using a wide array of weaponry against one another, and engaging in hand-to-hand combat between either humanlike characters or fantastical combatants. Becoming vicariously involved in graphic violence desensitizes children to actual violence. The more they see, the less shocking it is and the more acceptable it seems. This fact doesn't mean that they will act out what they have seen. Rather, violence is being done to the child's spirit.

There is a place for appropriate depictions of violence in storytelling, but acts of violence can be shown without focusing on the *graphic* part of the violence. The TBN video series *Gettysburg* is a good example of a war movie that portrays the violence of war convincingly but without graphic excess. I want my boys to see that kind of film to better grasp both the horrors and heroes of that conflict.

Your role is to sensitively discern how much violence is too much for your children at any particular age. Violent images will stay in your children's minds, so be careful for their sakes what you allow them to see. Take the time to preview films with which you are unfamiliar before allowing your children to watch them.

Casual Sexuality

The sexual revolution of the sixties didn't liberate anyone. Instead, it ushered in lowered standards and the heightened glorification of promiscuity and perversion. It also expanded the exploitation of women and men as mere physical bodies, not the precious creations of a loving God. The kinds of behavior that once were associated with broken lives and that brought about great shame are now an unending source of material for comedy and drama. What once was abnormal is being portrayed as normal and even preferred. And there is a trickle-down effect on children's programming, where sexual themes are "sensitively" explored (teen pregnancy, sexual abuse, AIDS, homosexuality) or subtly exploited (sexual temptation and failure, romanticized teen attraction, sensual dress and behavior). And then there's advertising!

This is the most difficult theme to monitor in your child's life because it is so pervasive. Sexuality permeates every form of media. Because it's inescapable, it is impossible to completely prevent exposure short of locking your kids in the house, shutting off the electricity, and never letting them out. In this case, the best defense is a good offense. Teach your children early about moral purity and train them to be self-governing. Exercising protective discipline will mean being selective about what is watched and when, and certainly avoiding any themes that make light of sexual practices that

God has deemed sinful or perverse. Of course, you will want to take extreme protective measures when it comes to the Internet and e-mail in order to protect your children's hearts and minds. Use a software filter or a filtered Internet service provider (ISP) to prevent accidental exposure to pornographic and other sexual sites when your children use the Internet. The risk of exposure to porn through e-mail spam is especially high unless you use an ISP with parental controls or some other type of e-mail filter. One e-mail message is all it takes to introduce your child to images even an adult should not see.[5]

Dysfunctional Lifestyles

This theme of the media encompasses alternative lifestyles, dysfunctional families, and broken people. The media highlight the unusual and atypical at the expense of the traditional nuclear family. The result is that every kind of nontraditional lifestyle that Scripture might see as broken and in need of redemption is made culturally normative. Meanwhile we see ridicule and marginalization of the intact, healthy Christian family, which is often portrayed as being extreme and out of touch with reality. Though few and far between, there are bright spots to be savored and enjoyed that celebrate God's design for the family and show the dangers of rejecting that design.

It's difficult to monitor your children's exposure to antifamily messages because they are so pervasive. But if you are reading a newspaper or watching a program on television and this bias does pop up, even subtly, take the opportunity to discuss with your child God's design for marriage and family as well as the destructive effects of sin. Don't let your silence inadvertently endorse views of life and morality that contradict biblical truth. Your children need to be reminded often that the happy and seemingly "normal" alternative and dysfunctional lives portrayed by media are a deliberate distortion of reality. Satan is using the media to promote his agenda, and your children need your protection to avoid absorbing the lie that all lifestyle choices are equally valid.

Coarse Language

Not only has our society seen a decline in common civility, but we have also witnessed the coarsening of language. The mass media are the leading influences in the use of foul, offensive, demeaning, and irreverent language. In fact, your children could hear more bad language from the media than they do at school or in the neighborhood. But harmful language doesn't stop with inappropriate words. It also encompasses making fun of individuals or groups of people (conflict humor), ethnic slurs, sexual innuendo, slang, sarcasm, name-calling, and much more. The effect in your child's heart will be a gradual desensitization to bad language and a heightened tolerance of it. It is a force that contradicts God's clear commands that our speech should be edifying, encouraging, and loving.

It is next to impossible to avoid exposure to mild profanities and crude slang in today's media, but that is not the real problem. The greater negative impact comes from the constant exposure to coarsened language, to undesirable attitudes that are expressed verbally, and even to patterns of speech. The words that come out of our mouths and the way we say them usually tells more about what we believe about God and the Bible—about what is in our hearts—than anything we do. Jesus taught that a person, whether good or evil, is known by his words (see Luke 6:44-45). Language patterns are established in childhood, so it's incumbent on us to protect our children from media influences that could have a long-term impact on their hearts and on their Christian testimony.

WHAT DOES CAPTURE YOUR CHILD'S IMAGINATION?

Because media messages are so pervasive, this area of protective discipline calls for spiritual discernment like no other. If you fail to protect your children from harmful messages and images, it's not a question of *whether* their imaginations will be influenced by the dark side of media, but *how much*.

How will the mixing of Christian truth and the supernatural themes of the media influence your children's views of spiritual reality? How will exposure to violence and coarse language influence their values about speech and humor? How will distorted sexual images and messages influence their attitudes toward the opposite sex, marriage, and family? Your children don't have the powers of discernment to reject on their own the barrage of unbiblical and ungodly themes that the media promote and defend. Children are vulnerable, which is why they need discerning parents to step in to protect them.

Someone might argue that a little bit of bad media can be good for children to help them learn discernment. I disagree. During the childhood years, parents must supply the discernment that children are too young to possess. Letting them watch a few of the most popular programs—which you know promote ungodly themes and messages—is like telling your kids that a "little sin" is all right now and then. If someone were to accuse me of being overprotective, I'd heartily agree. When I consider the nature of childhood as a time of innocence (see chapter 2), I picture myself standing over my children to protect them from harmful influences. As you listen to the Holy Spirit for help in discerning what is right and wrong for your children, don't be afraid to be overprotective. That can be a good thing if it's done for the right reasons. If you stand over your children to protect them now, when they reach their teen years they'll have a clear standard in their minds because of your directive discipline. And, more than that, they'll have pure hearts and minds because of your protective discipline. Discernment will come from the Holy Spirit as He enters their prepared hearts to help them apply the Word of God that you have instilled there. It won't come from peeking into the darkness to see what it's like.

The apostle Paul asked the Christians of Corinth, "For what partnership have righteousness and lawlessness, or what fellowship has light with darkness?" (2 Corinthians 6:14). The unspoken answer is straightforward: *None.* Paul was writing to adults, but he said, "I speak as to children" in making his point clear—light and darkness can't coexist in the same heart in the same way. He was reflecting the teaching of Jesus from the Sermon on the Mount: "No one can serve two masters; for either he will hate the one and love the other, or he will be devoted to one and despise the other. You cannot serve God and wealth" (Matthew 6:24). You can't serve God and the world at the same time. It's not possible to serve both light and darkness.

Perhaps an even more revealing way to consider the difference between light and darkness is to look at today's media content through the lens of the Ten Commandments (Exodus 20:1-17) and ask one question: "Which of God's commandments are being honored by the media that entertain and inform my children?" This question will heighten your awareness of just how far the Information Age has drifted from God's standards. If you can find media content for your children that honors and affirms *any* of the commandments, consider it a good find. I'm not arguing for entertainment with absolutely no depiction of sin—sinless entertainment wouldn't be entertaining. And for good to prevail in a story, you've got to have a good guy *and* a bad guy. What we're looking for is programming that doesn't glorify and exploit the sin that it depicts, but rather shows the painful fallout of breaking God's law. The issue is not whether sin is depicted, but how it's depicted.

The old adage about impure thoughts, usually attributed to Martin Luther, is that you can't keep the birds from flying around your head, but you can keep them from building a nest in your hair. Your children need you to help them shoo away the dark birds of the media so they won't nest in their hair. That task alone will make up the lion's share of your responsibility to exercise protective discipline in your child's life in the area of media. But if you do it well, you'll give your children a gift few children in today's culture will experience—a pure heart, unadulterated by the adult world. That's worth working for.

THE PROMISE OF
HEARTFELT DISCIPLINE

Setting Your Child's Feet on the Path of Life

My family enjoys car trips. They are great opportunities to listen to long audiobooks in one sitting—Dickens novels, C. S. Lewis's *The Chronicles of Narnia,* radio theatre. The last time we hit the road, though, we listened to something different—the audiobook version of *Apollo 13,* with added "I was there" comments by Jim Lovell, captain of the ill-fated lunar mission.

I was fascinated by Lovell's account of the point in the story after they had circled the moon and begun the return leg of their aborted lunar mission. Something was slowly pushing their wounded craft off course, and they had to use their limited fuel to fire guidance rockets to restore the proper trajectory. It would require both technology, primitive by today's standards, and jet pilot instincts. Because they were still far from earth, there was little room for error or bad timing. A few feet this way or that would mean certain death, either burning up on re-entry or careening off the atmosphere back into deep space. Their only hope for reaching home was to get back on the right path and stay there.

As Lovell explained what it took to return safely from that space flight, he was also drawing a picture of the task of Christian parenting. It provides a beautiful parallel to the biblical picture of discipline, to walking the path of life with your child in order to keep both of you on course and headed toward God. We, too, are far from home, and the tolerance for error is small. Choices made now that may seem unimportant are setting a trajectory that could either lead your children home to life or send them off into darkness and death. We have biblical instruction to guide us, but God also expects us to use our spiritual instincts, in the power of the Holy Spirit, to keep our children on His path.

This lifelong journey is not what most of us picture when we hear the word *discipline.* The Bible's picture of discipline is a mission as exciting and intense as piloting a spacecraft back to earth. Biblical discipline is not only the process of children's being trained by their parents, but it also is a complete lifestyle, a journey through life with God as the ultimate destination. It's not a method or formula or set of rules. It's a relationship in which one person leads another to follow God and to walk in His ways. Correcting sin and disobedience is a part of the process, but only a part. Biblical childhood discipline encompasses not just correction, but also direction and protection in equal measure.

The heart of childhood discipline is captured in a vivid image from the book of Proverbs: the path of life, the path of righteousness. Parents are the godly guides for their children. God has given us the privilege of lovingly directing each child along the path of life; correcting them when they sin by wandering off the path; and protecting them from influences that would lead them off the path.

As parents we already know the trail, so we can lead our children along the way. We know the wisdom and instruction contained in God's written Trail Guide, so we can guide and instruct our children on the rules of the trail. We also know the dangers that lie ahead, so we can protect our children from harmful forces and influences. Heartfelt discipline involves learning how to be the best guides we can be.

THE OUTCOME OF HEARTFELT DISCIPLINE

As I finish writing this chapter, my family is preparing to attend a Clarkson family reunion in another state. Several years ago when I started looking into our family heritage, I discovered a rich vein of faith that I hadn't known about. I learned that I am the tenth-generation descendant of Scottish cleric Thomas Boston. I found his writings and memoirs still in print and discovered that there is a statue in his honor in a Scotland churchyard. He was a great man of faith who took uncompromising stands for doctrines he believed in during the early 1700s. I read his memoirs and the notes about some of his sons and grandsons who continued in ministry. One recorded in his will a prayer for future generations of Boston descendants. When the family immigrated to America in the late 1700s (it had become the Clarkson line by then), their continued faith produced pastors, Civil War heroes, and state Supreme Court justices who spoke publicly of their faith in Christ. It is the descendants of that line who will gather to celebrate our shared heritage.

As I have uncovered the faith of these long-forgotten ancestors, I am reminded that my life is not defined by my birth date and my burial date. It's defined by the heritage that I claim from the past and that I pass on to succeeding generations. Some parents view their children as temporary responsibilities, having them for a while and then letting them go, trusting that they will find their way in life. Other parents, though, have discovered the biblical truth that they walk together with their children along a single path. It is covered with the footprints of those who have gone before them, and it stretches from one generation to the next and on into a future of children yet to be born.

That is what Psalm 78 describes. The fathers have taught the things of God to their children, and the psalmist proclaimed, "We will not conceal them from their children, but tell to the generation to come the praises of the LORD, and His strength and His wondrous works that He has done" (verse 4). God has given His truths to the parents so that "they should teach them to their children" (verse 5). This is putting children on the path of life. And why should parents do this? "That the generation to come might know, *even the children yet to be born,* that they may arise and tell them to *their* children" (verse 6).

Parenting is all about passing on faith not just to the next generation, but to the unseen generations yet to come. These are the unchanging truths that "they should put their confidence in God and not forget the works of God, but keep His commandments" (verse 7). The heart of parenting is not just about raising an obedient, well-behaved child, but about shaping your child's heart to follow God and placing his feet on the same path of life that you and those before you have walked. Your faith and teaching will live on in generations to come through the hearts of your children, and their children, who hear the call of God to "follow Me."

Heartfelt discipline also helps you see what God is doing through the hearts that He has changed and is changing, both yours and your child's. It's not a list of how-tos but a vision of why-tos. Heartfelt discipline is not a method of discipline, but a vision for discipline. True biblical discipline is a strategic relationship with your child. There is no formula or set of rules to follow. The "method" comes from the Holy Spirit, who lives within your heart to help you parent your children well as you walk with Him.

Heartfelt discipline will lift your vision to see not just the challenges and rewards of parenting that lie ahead, but the presence of God beside you with each step you take with your children. If you've ever walked a mountain trail, you know how much wonderful scenery you miss if all you do is look down at the trail. Unfortunately, many parents are missing the real joy of walking the path of life because they agonize over every step they take with their children. But God wants you to get your focus off your feet and instead look up and ahead to see where you're really going. It is only then that you discover the beauty and meaning that come with walking His path.

WALKING THE PATH OF LIFE

Here's an easy way to lift your eyes and begin to walk the path of life with your children in a way that will matter, both now and for eternity. There are four things you can do to begin moving toward heartfelt discipline, and you can use the acronym PATH to remember those actions.

P—Pray for Your Children Regularly

We have become so accustomed to thinking about discipline in terms of methods and formulas that we lose sight of the relational nature of discipline. Our first thoughts when a child needs to be corrected are "What should I do?" when they should be "What is God doing?" Prayer is one spiritual grace that forces us to bring God into the picture. Once you begin praying regularly for your children—for God to work in their hearts and minds—you can no longer approach childhood discipline as a formula to be followed. If you aren't praying, then your natural response is to rely on your own strength. But if you've been praying regularly, then you know that God is at work in your child and that He is at work in you through the Holy Spirit.

Praying is a way of affirming the wisdom that Solomon was passing on to his son in Proverbs 3:5-6. "Trust in the LORD with all your heart and do not lean on your own understanding. In all your ways acknowledge Him, and He will make your paths straight." This is essential wisdom for parents. First, we must turn to God and, from our hearts, give Him our trust. I can't do that without going to Him in prayer. Then we turn away from trying to be parents in our own power, doing it all based on natural ability or someone else's formula. We repent of trying to discipline our children without God. Then, in all the details of discipline, we recognize God's presence and ask for His guidance. We "acknowledge Him" through prayer, affirming our belief and trust in Him and asking Him to intervene. Then, as Solomon had learned, we can be confident that God will direct us in our desire to discipline our children biblically.

When I pray for my children, it changes how I look at them. Perhaps it opens what Paul called the "eyes" of my heart (see Ephesians 1:18). When I exercise discipline, it's no longer about whether I'll look good as a parent. When I pray regularly for them, I begin to see my children as spiritual beings and my discipline as a partnership with God to direct my children's heart to Him.

Praying "regularly" (see 1 Thessalonians 5:16-18) doesn't mean checking off a prayer list once a day. It is instead pursuing prayer as a way of life. It is developing the habit of praying throughout the day whenever God puts a child on your heart, or praying about a difficult heart attitude in a child, or praying for your own ability to show love and grace to a child to fill up his emotional tank. It also means taking the time to pray regularly for your children's future life pursuits, for their future spouses, and for how God can use them. In all your prayers, you are not just asking for God's help in discipline, but you are helping to build the spiritual heritage that is described in Psalm 78. You're putting your children's feet on the path of life, both for their own welfare and for the generations that follow.

A—Accept Your Children Unconditionally

God designed us to love our children. It's not something we have to learn how to do. But in addition to loving our children, do we accept them? It's not always easy to accept our children's personality traits, habits, quirks, and attitudes. It's one thing to love and hug them in a warm embrace, but quite another to accept them when they are cranky, resistant, loud, or moody. If we were honest with ourselves, we'd admit that at least some of our discipline originates from our difficulty in accepting our children the way God has made them. I'm convinced that the more we can learn to accept our children, the less we will find ourselves exercising corrective discipline and the more we will find ourselves just loving them into obedience.

Years ago Sally and I researched a valid system of identifying personality types. It helped us understand each other better, and then it helped us understand our children. But you don't have to buy into one personality model or another to understand that God has designed each of your children with specific traits, preferences, and motivations and that He wants you to accept everything about every one of your children just as He accepts them. That is the essence of unconditional love. You can trust that whatever personality God designed for your children is right, even when those traits and preferences clash with your own. Each child is a "gift of the LORD" to you, and even a "reward" (Psalm 127:3). By accepting everything about them, you are thanking God for His gift to you.

T—Teach and Train Your Children Diligently

Teaching and training make up the heart of your relationship with your children. The key parenting passages in both the Old Testament (Deuteronomy 6:4-9) and the New Testament (Ephesians 6:4) affirm both of these priorities of discipline. Teaching and training are like the two beats of the heart—one going in, the other going out. Teaching is the internalization of truth—taking it into the heart. Training is the externalization of truth—expressing outwardly what is in the heart. And, like a heartbeat, you can't have one without the other.

It's easy, though, for one or the other of these priorities to become formalized and then formula-ized. When that happens, your teaching is reduced to formal lessons, and your training is limited to mostly corrective discipline. But that is a far cry from the relational picture of discipline that we see in Scripture. It's the relationship between you and your child that will determine the effectiveness of your discipline. So work hard at maintaining the relational dynamics involved in teaching and training.

Picture yourself as a godly guide on the path of life, putting your arm around your child as you walk and talk about the life of God. Rather than relying on formal lessons, let your teaching become an ongoing conversation in which the Scriptures are a large part of the dialogue. Teach with your child's heart in view. Rather than strict corrective discipline, let your training find its power in your relationship with your child and in the power of the Holy Spirit. Remember that hiking a trail takes time, and so does heartfelt discipline. It will take more time to really relate to your child when instruction and discipline are needed, but it will result in a much greater effect and reward.

H—Honor Your Children Purposefully

Nobody likes to be corrected, since every instance of correction comes with the hidden message, "You messed up. You're not as good as you thought you were." There is a spirit-deadening realization of your own failure and a feeling of unworthiness. But all that can be neutralized when the correction comes from someone who has, many times before, affirmed your value and worth, recognized your efforts and good qualities, and encouraged and built you up in the Lord. In a word, when that person has honored you.

More than flattery and feel-good, self-esteem messages, your children need to know that they have honor in your eyes. Paul exhorted the Romans to "be devoted to one another in brotherly love; give preference to one another in honor" (Romans 12:10). The word *honor* means "to assign a value or a price," "to determine worth." As parents, you have the power to give your children a sense of self-worth or value, not just reflected in your eyes, but also in God's eyes. When you give your children honor, it will have a lifelong impact on them. You can "give preference" to them when you notice them, affirm their strengths, admire even their small accomplishments, appreciate their personalities, and believe in their dreams. You also do that when you tell them how loved they are by God and how God will never forsake them. They need to hear many times how valuable they are to you as well as how valuable they are to God.

The honor you give to your children will pay enormous dividends. By honoring them, you are strengthening the heart-bonds of relationship, which make up the heart of your discipline. But most of all you are giving them reasons to want to walk with you on the path of life, wherever you lead them and whether you are correcting, directing, or protecting them as you go. Honor will make your discipline heartfelt.

KEEP WALKING ON THE PATH OF LIFE

With the picture of heartfelt discipline before our eyes, we can discard outdated and unbiblical views of discipline. We can begin to discover a new sense of freedom in our parenting as we understand what it means to parent in the power of the Holy Spirit.

There is no more important task in your life than the task of setting your children's feet on the path of life. They are God's gift and reward to you in this life, and they are your gift to the world. But there is an eternal reward to parenting. Through your children, God has given you the privilege of passing on your faith and the truth of Scripture to future generations. When you reach your heavenly home and stand before God, He will be waiting to show you the generations after you that will find His path to their eternal home because of what you did for your children. As you learn the ways of heartfelt discipline, may you enjoy God's favor, know His presence, and walk every day in the power of His Spirit as you guide your children home to God along the path of life.

NOTES

Introduction

1. If you are seeking additional input on specific how-to approaches to childhood discipline, please see "Recommended Resources" beginning on page 241.

Chapter 1

1. Jesus commonly used parables to teach divine truth or ideas by means of illustration and story rather than by direct instruction. The details of the parable are often used to help make the point, but not necessarily to teach specific truths. In the parable of the sower, Jesus describes different kinds of ground where the seed falls, only one of which bears fruit. However, He is not saying that these nonfruitful grounds are the only other kinds of hearts in the world, that those hearts will never be able to believe, or that only the heart with "prepared soil" can hear and respond to the gospel. His point is simply that the seed of God's word, the gospel of the kingdom and salvation, will take root when it falls into the soil of a prepared heart.

Chapter 2

1. In 2 Kings 2:23-25, the *King James Version* refers to "little children" who are cursed by the prophet Elisha and subsequently mauled by bears. However, these were not young children but *naar,* a Hebrew word that refers to young men. They were rowdy teenagers, not little children.

2. For more on the mystery of the gospel, see Romans 16:25-27 and Colossians 2:1-3.

Chapter 3

1. See Proverbs 13:24.

2. See *Theological Wordbook of the Old Testament*, vol. 1, ed. R. L. Harris et al. (Chicago: Moody, 1980), 249.

3. See *Expositor's Bible Commentary*, vol. 5, ed. Frank E. Gaebelein (Grand Rapids, Mich.: Zondervan, 1991), 1061.

4. These four verses clearly refer to foolish adults. However, some teachers argue that the "fool" in these passages becomes parallel to the "child" in other rod passages. The arguments they use to apply these verses to spanking children don't hold up.

    First, "back" is not the same as "backside." The Hebrew word used in Proverbs 10:13 and 26:3 is consistently translated "back" in other passages, never "backside." It pictures a slave who is beaten on the back by a master in order to force the slave to bow his head in submission to authority. Proverbs 14:3 uses a different Hebrew word that is translated "pride" in the eighteen other verses where it appears. Pride, which could describe the refusal to bow the head to proper authority, brings a self-inflicted rod to the foolish.

    Second, the rod mentioned in these four verses is not just a switch or small branch. At the time of the writing of Proverbs, *shebet* was commonly understood to be an instrument used to inflict pain. The idea of the rod being more of a small "switch" comes from Proverbs 14:3, where the Hebrew word *choter* is translated "rod." It is used only one other time, in Isaiah 11:1: "a *shoot* will spring from the stem of Jesse." The *choter* is a twig coming out of a branch. Based on this verse, some extrapolate that the rod in Proverbs is really a twig or a switch. In contrast, Ezekiel 19:11 indicates that a ruler's scepter (his *shebet*) was made from "strong branches" of a vine (literally, "rods of strength"). It pictures a heavy staff, even a club.

    Finally, the rod is not meant to be interpreted symbolically in these four passages. There's no question that the term *shebet* is used elsewhere to symbolize God's punishment or judgment. However, nothing in Proverbs 10:13 and 26:3 suggests a symbolic meaning. Even in Proverbs 22:8, a physical rod is depicted within the metaphor "rod of his fury." The plain reading and understanding of these four verses is that a foolish man needs to be whacked on the back with a real, pain-inducing rod to force him to submit to authority and wisdom.

5. A different Hebrew word, *naarah,* denotes a young woman. Also, *noar* denotes youth in general. However, it could be that *naar* refers to both young men and young women in some verses of Scripture. Typically, though, *naar* is meant to be understood as a young man. It may be that the underlying principles of these verses hold true for all youth, male or female.

6. As we consider the Old Testament teachings on the rod, you might be wondering, *But what about Hebrews 12:4-11?* In that passage, the writer states unambiguously that suffering is one of the ways God disciplines us for our good, just as fathers discipline their sons. Since this passage includes the line "and scourges [whips] every son whom He receives" (verse 6), many quote it as a New Testament justification for the physical discipline of young children. But consider the following points:

    a) The Hebrews passage is addressed to adults and is not really about earthly parental discipline, but about the discipline that God carries out in response to His children's disobedience.

    b) There is no direct exhortation or instruction in this passage to fathers about their sons. Instead, the passage uses the father-son relationship to illustrate God's use of suffering to discipline us.

    c) Proverbs 3:12, the passage quoted in Hebrews, was addressing the young man and not a young child. Therefore, the Hebrews passage should be understood in the same light, as speaking of fathers disciplining sons who are young men.

    d) Since both Roman law and rabbinical law considered young children to be without any rights, it makes more sense that this passage is speaking of young men whose fathers discipline them out of love so that they will choose to share in God's holiness, which is a right they now enjoy.

e) The reference to being "subject to the Father" (verse 9) in order to live is an echo of the proverb that discipline will prevent the premature death of a young man (23:13).

f) It seems unlikely that a young child would be able to understand that suffering and discipline are good because they produce the "peaceful fruit of righteousness" (verse 11), a concept more in keeping with maturity.

Chapter 4

1. See Romans 7:5; 8:5-8; Galatians 5:16-17.
2. See Genesis 15:6; Habakkuk 2:4; Romans 4; Galatians 3:6-9.
3. See Luke 8:4-15. For a more complete discussion of this parable, see chapter 1 of this book.

Chapter 5

1. See Matthew 5:21-48; John 1:17; Romans 4:16, 5:20.
2. H. Clay Trumbull, *Hints on Child Training* (Philadelphia: John D. Wattles, 1890, 1893), 247, 250-1.
3. J. C. Ryle, *The Upper Room* (London: Banner of Truth Trust, 1970), 285.
4. The Greek root *sym* means "with," and *pathos* means "feeling."
5. Some will cite Hebrews 12 as a biblical justification for the practice of strict discipline. However, as discussed in chapter 3 of this book, the Hebrews passage does not address young children, and neither does it constitute a direct command or clear mandate to parents. Instead, it uses a reality of Old Testament Jewish life to illustrate God's discipline of His adult children.

6. Gary Chapman and Ross Campbell, M.D., *The Five Love Languages of Children* (Chicago: Moody, 1997), 20. The five love languages are physical touch, words of affirmation, quality time, gifts, and acts of service.

7. For more on these personality types, see Clay Clarkson, *Educating the WholeHearted Child* (Walnut Springs, Tex.: Whole Heart, 1996).

Chapter 6

1. For a more complete discussion of these influences, see part 4 of this book, "Protective Discipline."

Chapter 7

1. This family devotional outline is explained more fully in Clay Clarkson, *Our 24 Family Ways,* rev. ed. (Walnut Springs, Tex.: Whole Heart, 2003).

Chapter 8

1. Additional passages that stress a parent's responsibility to instruct his or her children are listed here:

Deuteronomy 31:12-13: "Assemble the people, the men and the women and children and the alien who is in your town, *so that they may hear and learn and fear the* LORD *your God,* and be careful to observe all the words of this law. Their children, who have not known, will hear and *learn to fear* the LORD your God, as long as you live on the land which you are about to cross the Jordan to possess."

Psalm 78:4-7: "We will not conceal them from their children, but *tell to the generation to come* the praises of the LORD, and His strength and His wondrous works that He has done. For He established a testimony in Jacob and appointed a law in Israel, *which He commanded our fathers that they should teach them to their children,* that the generation to come might know, even the children yet to be born, that they may arise and *tell them to their children,* that they should put their confidence in God and not forget the works of God, but keep His commandments."

Proverbs (selected verses): "Hear, my son, *your father's instruction* and do not forsake *your mother's teaching"* (1:8).

"My son, *do not forget my teaching,* but let your heart keep my commandments" (3:1).

"Hear, O sons, *the instruction of a father,* and give attention that you may gain understanding, for I give you *sound teaching,* do not abandon *my instruction"* (4:1-2).

2. Lawrence O. Richards, *Expository Dictionary of Bible Words* (Grand Rapids, Mich.: Zondervan, 1985), 589.

3. For more on asking questions that elicit rich discussion, see Clay Clarkson, *Educating the WholeHearted Child* (Walnut Springs, Tex.: Whole Heart, 1996).

Chapter 9

1. Several books have wonderfully expanded this idea and even applied it to children and families. See "Recommended Resources" beginning on page 241 for a listing of useful resources.

Chapter 10

1. Lawrence O. Richards, *Expository Dictionary of Bible Words* (Grand Rapids, Mich.: Zondervan, 1985), 190.

2. For a review of directive discipline, see chapters 5 through 8 of this book.

3. For help in finding verses that apply to common discipline situations, I recommend Kara Durbin, *Parenting with Scripture* (Chicago: Moody, 2001). This topical guide for parents can be a great help in finding the right scriptures to apply to a situation. In addition, topical Bibles and concordances will help you find the most applicable verses.

Chapter 11

1. H. Clay Trumbull, *Hints on Child Training* (Philadelphia: John D. Wattles, 1890, 1893), 10-1.

2. Ross Campbell, M.D., *Relational Parenting* (Chicago: Moody, 2000), 12.

3. For more on honor-based parenting, see Scott Turansky and Joanne Miller, *Say Goodbye to Whining, Complaining, and Bad Attitudes...in You and Your Kids!* (Colorado Springs: Shaw, 2000). The book is filled with practical tips and solid advice on honor and discipline.

Chapter 12

1. For the punishment of Israel, see Psalm 89:30-32 and Lamentations 3:1-3. For the use of the rod against other nations, see Psalm 2:7-9 and Revelation 19:15.

2. See Hebrews 12:7-11.

3. Many mature Christians are convinced that physical discipline of children is unnecessary at best and unbiblical at worst. If you are interested in the case against spanking and hitting, you will find it argued best by Dr. William Sears, a pediatrician, the author of twenty-seven books, and father of eight children, whose Christian convictions come through in everything he writes. In *The Discipline Book: How to Have a Better Behaved Child from Birth to Age Ten* (New York: Little Brown, 1995), Dr. Sears and his wife, Martha, a registered nurse, provide convincing reasons to reject the spanking model in favor of an "attachment parenting" model based on "building the right relationship with your child." Their book is the best how-to manual on childhood discipline available, applying their model to every imaginable situation for children. Their other books, including *The Successful Child: What Parents Can Do to Help Kids Turn Out Well* (New York: Little Brown, 2002), cover all aspects of having and raising children, as does their Web site, www.askdrsears.com.

Chapter 13

1. Gladys M. Hunt, *Honey for a Child's Heart* (Grand Rapids, Mich.: Zondervan, 1969, 1978, 1989, 2002), 21.

2. *The American Heritage Dictionary of the English Language,* 4th ed. (Boston: Houghton Mifflin, 2000). Found at www.dictionary.com.

Chapter 14

1. See Deuteronomy 6:4-9 and Ephesians 6:4.

2. H. Clay Trumbull, *Hints on Child-Training* (Philadelphia: John D. Wattles, 1890, 1893), 201-4.

3. Dan Adams, *The Child Influencers* (Cuyahoga Falls, Ohio: Home Team, 1990), 113.

4. Ross Campbell, M.D., *Relational Parenting* (Chicago: Moody, 2000), 52.

5. See Ephesians 6:4; 1 Thessalonians 2:11-12; 2 Timothy 3:14-15.

Chapter 15

1. Michael D. O'Brien, *A Landscape with Dragons* (Fort Collins, Colo.: Ignatius, 1998), 67.

2. O'Brien, *Dragons,* 68.

3. O'Brien, *Dragons,* 45.

4. See Leviticus 19:31; Deuteronomy 18:9-14; 2 Kings 21:6; Revelation 21:8.

5. Filtering software includes programs such as CYBERsitter, CyberPatrol, and Net Nanny. Filtered ISPs include Integrity Online, LifeLineNet, MayberryUSA, and Family Click. E-mail spam filters and controls include AOL Parental Controls, Earthlink Spaminator, Spamkiller, and Spam Buster.

RECOMMENDED RESOURCES

Parenting/Discipline

The Discipline Book, Dr. William Sears (Little Brown, 1995). Sears is a
Christian father of eight and a nationally known pediatrician and author.
This fact-filled book could be a how-to manual for many aspects of heart-
felt discipline.

Hints on Child Training, H. Clay Trumbull (Great Expectations Press, 1890).
Trumbull, a Christian leader, prolific author, and father of eight, wrote this
book to answer a friend's question about how he raised godly children.

The Mission of Motherhood, Sally Clarkson (WaterBrook Press, 2003). I highly
recommend this inspirational portrait of biblical motherhood from the
mother of my children. She shows why and how God's greatest blessings
are found in the traditional, biblical view of motherhood.

Relational Parenting, Ross Campbell, M.D. (Moody Press, 2000). Campbell
rightly identifies the heart of childhood discipline as a relationship between
parents and their children. I highly recommend this book for all parents.

Directive Discipline

Celebrations That Touch the Heart, Brenda Poinsett (WaterBrook Press, 2001).
These faith-filled, heart-touching ideas and proven advice from a seasoned
mother of three children will help you keep the heart of Christ in your
holiday celebrations.

The Five Love Languages of Children, Gary Chapman and Ross Campbell, M.D.
(Moody Press, 1997). Everyone in your family will benefit from these
simple yet profound insights on how to communicate love to your children
in a way that they will receive it best and that will meet their deepest emotional needs.

Journeys of Faithfulness, Sarah Clarkson (Whole Heart Press, 2002). My seventeen-year-old daughter wrote this inspirational devotional book for other "faithful girls." It is a series of fictional retellings of biblical stories about four young women in Scripture.

Our 24 Family Ways, revised edition, Clay Clarkson (Whole Heart Press, 2003). This illustrated family devotional and discipleship resource is built around twenty-four statements of family values, with 120 fully outlined Bible devotions.

Praying the Bible with Your Family, David and Heather Kopp (WaterBrook Press, 2000). The Kopps combine Bible reading and prayer in family devotions. Their book offers child-friendly activities and actual prayers in a story-oriented devotional format. It puts God's words into your prayers.

Corrective Discipline

Parenting with Scripture, Kara Durbin (Moody Press, 2001). This easy-to-use "topical guide for teachable moments" covers one hundred common childhood and teen topics with selected verses, discussion points, activities, and action ideas.

Praying the Bible for Your Children, David and Heather Kopp (WaterBrook Press, 1997). This is a wonderful resource for praying the actual words of Scripture for your children. The Kopps, parents of five, provide 122 Scripture-based prayers.

Say Goodbye to Whining, Complaining, and Bad Attitudes…in You and Your Kids! Scott Turansky and Joanne Miller (Shaw Books, 2000). This is really a book on how to show honor to your children. The authors provide lots of practical, how-to advice with examples to help you reach your child's heart.

Protective Discipline

The Child Influencers, Dan Adams (Home Team Press, 1990). The author offers an easy-to-read but penetrating analysis of the drift away from family-based influences in a child's life. He also addresses the negative impact of cultural influences on a child's heart.

Honey for a Child's Heart, Gladys M. Hunt (Zondervan, 2002). This classic work on "the imaginative use of books in family life" includes an annotated list of the best books for children up to age fourteen.

These and other heart-building, faith-strengthening books and resources are available from the Whole Heart Online Bookstore. Whole Heart Ministries is dedicated to strengthening your family to follow God wholeheartedly. For more information, please visit our Web site:

Whole Heart Ministries
www.wholeheart.org
mail@wholeheart.org